A PROMISE OF BEAUTY

A PROMISE OF BEAUTY
THE OCTAGON TOWER AND LANTERN AT ELY CATHEDRAL

MICHAEL WHITE

FRAMECHARGE PRESS

ISBN: 978-0-9555777-0-3

British Library Cataloguing in Publication Data. A catalogue record for this book is available from the British Library.

Published by: FrameCharge Press
                       PO Box 238
                       Ely, UK
                       CB7 9BR
                       editor@framecharge.com
                       http://www.framecharge.com

Photography: Michael White
Technical Editor: Peter White
Editor/Designer: Jeff White

Software
  Page Layout: Scribus 1.3.3.6
  Image Manipulation: GIMP 2.2.14
                       Krita 1.6.2
  Operating System: Fedora Core 6 Linux

Printed and bound by Cambrian Printers Ltd, Aberystwyth, Wales

10 9 8 7 6 5 4 3 2 1

Eely Minster

This presenteth it self afar off to the eye of the traveller, and on all sides at great distance, not onely maketh a promise, but giveth earnest of the beauty thereof.

Thomas Fuller, *The Worthies of England* (1662)

Author's Note

I came to Ely for the first time in 1997, not on my own account, but to assist my son in finding his first house; so I could say I discovered the city's many charms completely by accident. That reconnaissance of properties in Ely led directly to the purchase of our own house, and my retirement to Ely in 1998. I became a cathedral guide shortly after, at my wife's perspicacious prompting, and it seemed only a natural progression to 'higher things' when I became an Octagon tower guide in 2002.

When I began to look for information about the Octagon, the present central tower of Ely Cathedral, I found the going hard. No single source seemed to say very much in detail about the fall of the original Norman central tower in 1322, which so radically changed the centre of our cathedral. That was until, quite by chance, I found a copy of the Rev. D. J. Stewart's *On the Architectural History of Ely Cathedral* (1868) in the local antiques centre. The book had clearly never been read, because the pages were still uncut at the edges, and this added to the excitement, as I parted the pages to read the account of a true successor to Alan of Walsingham, the builder of the Octagon. Stewart had been the sacrist here at Ely in the nineteenth century. One drawback quickly became apparent; Stewart was quoting long passages of ancient Latin from the mediaeval sacrist's records with the aplomb of a Victorian who clearly felt that the serious student would not need a translation!

Thus, I quickly became re-acquainted with a Latin dictionary after a gap of forty-six years, and more to the point was introduced by Stewart to the sacrist rolls, compiled by Alan of Walsingham during his time as sacrist. The surviving rolls (there are nine years or so missing from the relevant twenty-year period) detail the expenditure for some of the time the Octagon and Lantern were being built, and give tantalising glimpses of the craftsman who built them. We are told some of their Christian names, their wages, sometimes where they came from, but there is little information about how they built the Octagon. We can sometimes infer progress from the entries and materials purchased, but much of the mystery of how the great structure rose to such heights will always remain.

Sacrist Rolls of Ely (1908), edited by F. R. Chapman (another reverend gentleman), a rare book, but available in Ely Library (Cathedral Collection), provided notes and transcripts and a glossary, and saved a bit of 'Latin fatigue'.

A further impetus to my efforts came with my first reading of our own John Maddison's book *Ely Cathedral: Design and Meaning* (2000), and the various papers by Phillip Lindley as detailed in the bibliography.

Finally, I have been very fortunate that excellent guiding colleagues and patient members of the cathedral community have given me enormous help, whilst the searching questions of visitors have sparked new enquiries, fuelling more research, and so the quest continues.

My grateful thanks are due to the Dean and Chapter of Ely Cathedral, who afforded me every facility in my job as an Octagon guide to enable me to study and photograph the Octagon and Lantern at length. A further considerable debt of thanks is due to guiding colleagues Pam Blakeman and Ella Thurmott, who persevered through very primitive versions of my manuscript, and provided many helpful suggestions and additions, while others have volunteered vital facts from their own experience to enrich the final version here. I am also uniquely blessed as the nominal head of my little nuclear family, insofar as my dear wife provided the original impetus for this little book, and chivvied me gently all the way to completion, my youngest son introduced me so diplomatically to the tyranny of formal style standards for such works, while my eldest son has chiselled a polished article from the rough stone that I had originally quarried. It goes almost without saying of course, that any inaccuracies, mistakes or misunderstandings are my own unaided work.

I began to write this book in order to marshal the information I had gathered for use in my guided tours, but it rapidly acquired its own momentum. What follows then is a brief outline of the status quo in England and Ely in the early fourteenth century, and then a detailed account of the collapse of Ely's Norman crossing tower in 1322, and the subsequent construction of the Octagon tower and

Lantern. I then give full consideration to the impact of the major restorations of the eighteenth and nineteenth centuries, and outline the story up to the present day. There are further sections that deal with the statuary and stained glass of the Octagon. While much of my account is a rehearsal of the existing wisdom around Alan of Walsingham's creation, I hope the reader will agree that this study offers some new conjectures in areas that have caused differences between scholars in the past, most notably in the area of the Etheldreda sculptures on the columns around the crossing. The final sections offer a description of the Octagon and Lantern structures from 'within', in the hope that visitors will flock to visit this remarkable building. Some suggested answers to 'frequently asked questions' follow, together with a select bibliography.

All I hope is that my account will be considered, argued with, but hopefully not refuted. I am neither a civil engineer, nor an academic, and this account is a personal resumé of my reading and day-to-day experience as a guide here at Ely.

It seems curiously appropriate to have begun the enterprise on 12 February 2006, a mere 684 years almost to the day since Abbot Richard's stone tower fell in 1322.

I only hope that I have shown a tiny fraction of the energy, ingenuity, and staying power of those three great colleagues, Bishop Hotham, Prior Crauden, and of course Alan of Walsingham, the *flos operatorum* (flower of workmen), in completing my task.

I would like to demonstrate that in my view, the Octagon represents three resounding triumphs. Firstly, it was a triumph over great structural and financial difficulties. The construction effectively and beautifully mended the hole in the roof caused by the fall of the original stone tower in 1322.

Secondly, it was a triumph of co-operation and friendship. Hotham bore the costs of the refurbishment of the three bays of the choir to the east of the new Octagon, Prior Crauden began the successful management of the quite enormous debts of the monastery at that time, and Alan the Sacrist provided his not inconsiderable practical skills. Everything you read suggests close friendship and affection between the prime movers of the project. The cost of rebuilding the centre of the cathedral was met, in the main, by the monastery itself and by some voluntary contributions from folk outside the community.

Finally, above all, it was a triumph of innovation. The design of the stone Octagon tower and the revolutionary way the wooden Lantern is suspended inside it took forward the craft of carpentry

The Lantern, taken from Alan of Walsingham's grave slab in the nave

to new levels of attainment in the first half of the fourteenth century.

Somebody put together the suggestions of the masons and the carpenters, and produced the coherent design above us. Judging by the favourable comments of his colleagues at the time of the collapse, and later in his fulsome epitaph, it was Alan the Sacrist, who went on to fill the office of prior before he died in 1363.

> *These things of note are at Ely, the Lantern and Chapel of Mary,*
> *A windmill too, and a vineyard that yieldeth wine in abundance,*
> *Know that the choir before you exceedeth all others in beauty,*
> *Made by Alan our brother, Alan the wise master-builder;*
> *He who of craftsman the flower, was gifted with strength in his lifetime.*
> *Alan the Prior, forget not, here facing the Choir lieth buried.*
> *He, for that older Tower which fell one night in the darkness,*
> *Here erected, well-founded, the Tower ye now are beholding,*
> *Many the Houses of God that, as Prior and Sacrist he builded.*
> *May God grant him in Heaven a seat at the end of his labour.*

Edward Conybeare's abridged translation of Alan's epitaph in
Highways and Byways in Cambridge and Ely (London, Macmillan, 1910), p. 360.

Contents

Introduction

Any description of the fall of Ely Cathedral's Norman crossing tower in 1322, and its replacement with the famous Octagon tower and its Lantern, needs to be preceded by an account of the early history of the religious foundation, and some account of the geology and geography of the Isle of Ely. Alan of Walsingham included many references to that early history in his designs for his 'new work', which occupied the twenty years from 1322 to 1342.

Approaching the city across the flat fields of the reclaimed 'fens' that stretch the sixteen miles or so northwards up the A10 from Cambridge, one learns the basic geography of the place in one journey. The City of Ely, at an elevation of eighty-four feet (twenty-six metres), is situated on a low hill of clay, with a thin and insubstantial cap of 'lower greensand', a kind of sandstone. The Isle of Ely is about eight miles by seven in extent, with a small drained marsh in its centre, and its highest point is around ninety-eight feet (thirty metres) above sea level. For much of its history, up to the seventeenth century when determined attempts at draining began, the Isle of Ely was surrounded by huge marshes locally called 'fens' that extended from Cambridge as far north as Lincolnshire. The fens cover an approximate area of some 1300 square miles. To the south and west of the Isle the fens are peat fens, formed during periods of fresh water flooding in ancient times, whilst there are 'silt' fens to the northeast, formed during incursions by the sea in pre-history.

In the early seventh century, this huge morass with shifting watercourses, vast fisheries and limitless reed beds, formed the important western boundary of the Saxon kingdom of the East Angles. Its local chieftain Tondberht was selected by Anna, the King of East Anglia, as someone who should be drawn into an alliance to protect their mutual interests. Anna's daughter,

Opposite: A view of the choir, organ and presbytery

Æthelthryth (or Etheldreda to give her her Latinised name) was accordingly married off to Tondberht, receiving as her dowry the Isle of Ely, already a settlement of some significance with its own Christian church endowed with funds sent by Ethelbert the King of Kent. This political marriage, which was also loveless (at Etheldreda's insistence), lasted only two years or so before Tondberht died. Despite now owning the Isle in her own right, Etheldreda was not able to realise her long-held ambition to found a monastery there until after her second platonic and political marriage of alliance to Ecgfrith, the heir to the kingdom of Northumbria. He was eventually persuaded to allow her to become a nun, and after many adventures and miracles she evaded his attempts to take her back forcibly, coming south to found her community at Ely in AD 673.

Here the monastery for monks and nuns, in two very separate communities within the same monastery, found not only seclusion from the world but fertile farms on the Isle, limitless resources of food from the fens, and copious quantities of rushes, sedge and clay for building purposes. Good building stone was also available in the high ground to the northwest of the fens that could be transported to Ely by boat down the River Nene, across the Wash and up the Great Ouse.

Etheldreda's fame in the short period of six years or so she was Abbess of Ely grew as pilgrims became convinced of her holiness, purity and power, and many thousands of them began to make the difficult journey to the Isle of Ely. The market town of Ely began to grow at the gates of the monastery, and even today one can establish the northern boundary of the monastery simply by walking down the High Street. For much of its length the buildings on the south side are what remains of two departmental buildings of the monastery, i.e. the Almonry and the Sacrist's establishments.

Etheldreda's reputation as a powerful and popular saint has survived many vicissitudes down the years. In 870 the Vikings destroyed the monastery, but roughly one hundred years later the Saxon King Edgar, taking advantage of the peaceful period instituted by his reign as one of the first 'Kings of All England', reinstated the monastery as one of the Benedictine jewels of his new religious realm, with renewed benefactions and grants of land and estates. The legends and stories of Etheldreda received a new polish at this time, and her reputation as a saint was still so strong in 1072 that when the Normans finally captured the Isle, and dismantled the Saxon minster and monastery, they reinstated

Etheldreda and her three saintly relatives, Seaxburh, Ermenilda, and Withburga, in shrines at the east end of their new cathedral.

As the events of the fourteenth century unfold in the following pages we will see that the power of the St Etheldreda story was still firmly fixed at the forefront of the minds of the designers and craftsmen who built the Octagon. We will see represented in the fabric and statuary the life and miracles of St Etheldreda, and a deep reverence for the Saxon benefactors who reinstated the monastery in the tenth and eleventh centuries. If we piece together the evidence of lost windows and obscure carvings, I am convinced we can also detect a considerable gratitude to King Edgar, who seems to be recognised as the true founder of the Benedictine monastery through his ecclesiastical officers, the three saints, Ethelwold, Dunstan, and Oswald.

England in the Early Fourteenth Century

Edward II had been on the throne since 1307. His father, Edward I, had died that year in mid-campaign, on his way to teach the Scots another warlike lesson. Almost the first act of Edward II's new reign was to recall his proud favourite, Piers Gaveston, with whom he was hopelessly besotted, back from the Continent, where Edward I had exiled him.[1]

Under pressure from the King of France, Philip IV, who felt that his daughter Isabella, Edward's Queen, was being slighted by Gaveston's presence in the royal affections, the favourite was again exiled, this time more honourably as Viceroy of Ireland, in 1308. Returning to England in 1309, Gaveston had not learnt any lessons and by 1312 the baronial opposition to the favourite's preferment by Edward was on the point of becoming civil war. Thomas of Lancaster and the Earl of Warwick succeeded in isolating Gaveston from the King's forces and he was summarily executed on Blacklow Hill in Warwickshire. Edward never forgave the barons for slaughtering his 'brother',[2] and in grief formed the intention to seek revenge when the opportunity offered.

The years 1314 and 1315 were notable for their extremely bad weather and poor harvests. Throughout Europe there were many reports of severe famine. In Ireland, always seemingly on the edge of disaster in those times, there were reports that poor folk were eating dogs and—in one extreme report—each other. It took many communities a considerable time to regain lost ground after this lean period.

The comprehensive defeat by the Scots at the Battle of Bannockburn in 1314 was of course a complete disaster for Edward. He was certainly not his father's son in any warlike sense. It provided proof, if proof was needed, that Edward was not living up to the promise he had shown as Prince of Wales. The golden

Opposite: The west tower and the southwest transept from the south

1 See Alison Weir, *Isabella, She-wolf of France, Queen of England* (Pimlico, 2006), p. 40. Also Ian Mortimer, *The Greatest Traitor* (Pimlico, 2004), pp 32–50.

2 See Michael Prestwich, *The Three Edwards: War and State in England, 1272–1377* (London, Routledge, 2003), p. 72.

youth who had so many attractive and affable qualities had become the feckless and ineffectual king who was intent only on having his own way and favouring his chosen few. The lost battle also meant that the Scots now had free rein to plunder and despoil the North of England, and this they did with great success.

One major criticism levelled at Edward was that despite the many problems that beset his realm, he was not sufficiently interested in his regal duties, and preferred country pursuits like hedging and ditching, and manual tasks like working as a smith. In 1316 it is reported with great scorn by a chronicler that Edward spent several weeks in the fens 'on holiday' with a great gathering of the common folk, skating and sailing.

By 1320 Edward had two new favourites, Hugh de Spencer the Elder and his son, Hugh de Spencer the Younger. The rapacity of the regime instituted by Edward and his two favourites led to an uprising of the barons in 1321, which Edward succeeded in crushing at the Battle of Boroughbridge. In early 1322, about the time of Ely's collapse, the two ringleaders of that revolt, the Earl Mortimer of Chirk and Earl Mortimer of Wigmore, were languishing in the Tower, and Thomas of Lancaster had been executed. One chronicler said that the reign 'of horror piled on horror' had begun. Another said 'The harshness of the King has today increased so much that no-one however great or wise, dares to cross his will'.

The next five years would see the successful invasion of England by Edward's queen, Isabella, and her new lover Earl Mortimer of Wigmore, who had made a miraculous escape from the Tower to rejoin her on the Continent.

In 1327, Edward was forced to abdicate, and the traditional tale says that he met his end in particularly gruesome circumstances in Berkeley castle. (I note however that several historians now discount that rather lurid tale of his death at the hands of his gaolers, in favour of the version where Edward is allowed to escape from England and live out his days in a monastery in the Lombardy hills.[3])

One could say, without fear of contradiction, that England was not an entirely settled and peaceful place in which to undertake a major and costly building enterprise.

3 See Paul Doherty, *Isabella and the Strange Death of Edward II* (London, Robinson, 2003), pp 35–53. Also Alison Weir, *Isabella, She-wolf of France and Queen of England*, pp 279–294.

The Monastery at Ely in the Early Fourteenth Century

Between 1272, when Edward I had come to the throne, and the end of that century, the monastery had enjoyed a fairly calm if heavily taxed existence. When re-founded in AD 970, the complement of monks was intended to be seventy, and in the Chapter Ordinances of 1241 to 1254, the *primo provisum* ('first provision') laid down that this total was to be restored. The statutes of Ralph of Walpole in 1300 maintained this aim and said no suitable applicant should be turned away. In practice however, it seems that the total of monks in the community at the date of the collapse of the central tower was around fifty or so. S. J. A. Evans in his *Ely Chapter Ordinances and Visitation Records 1241-1515* (1940) suggests that from 1335 to 1353 the average number of monks was around forty-seven not including the prior. In 1349 when the Black Death arrived in Ely we know there were fifty-four monks, of whom only twenty-eight survived the epidemic.

The monastery itself, a very large and successful enterprise, which managed itself under the auspices of around ten department heads, had already succeeded in attracting a flourishing market town to its gates. In addition to the community of monks and senior officials, there would have been considerable numbers of lay brothers and servants to service the needs of the convent, and it is estimated that the entire monastery had a total complement of at least three hundred souls. The records of the various departments of the monastery even detail the different liveries to be worn by the servants of each head of department, and the larger departments had their own establishment buildings purpose-built for their use.

The monastery was largely self-sufficient in providing the staples necessary for its existence, even down to grading its produce to the rank of the consumer. The monastery bakeries produced at least five different grades of bread, from the finest *panes monachales* ('monks' bread') and *panes milites* ('soldiers' bread') for higher-ranking customers, down to *trencho* which were in fact thick stale crusts on which the lowest grade servants' dinners were served (the crusts became edible once they had absorbed some gravy). Purpose-built brew-houses brewed at least four kinds of beer, which were also provided according to status. *Bona* (good) was provided to high officials, *mediocris* (middle) to senior folk, and *debilis* (weak) to lower grade clerks. *Skegman*, for which no translation will perhaps be required, was provided for the monks who were allowed a generous daily allowance of this small beer. It was perhaps only slightly preferable to drinking the water available in Ely, which was indifferent in health terms to say the least. Food was plentiful, in that the surrounding marshes provided unlimited wildfowl, fish, and of course, eels. The farmland on the Isle and in the monastery's possessions on the mainland around the marsh was of good quality, and produce was abundant, while two vineyards on south-facing slopes provided wine for the Bishop and the monastery itself. Although the monks took vows of poverty, chastity and obedience, the Benedictines' unofficial motto was 'nothing harsh or hard to bear', and Ely feasts became a legend in their time.

Prices were rising quite fast by the standards of the times towards 1300 however, and King Edward I had placed quite heavy burdens of taxation on the monasteries to help finance his wars against the Scots. There are mentions too that Ely had been involved in litigation at Rome and that this had proved very costly. By far the community's biggest concern at the point immediately before the collapse of the tower, however, was the huge burden of debt the monastery had incurred. Prior John de Fressingfield had pursued an aggressive policy of trying to enlarge the estates of the monastery, but in doing so had incautiously run up debts which totalled £3,391 in 1321.[4]

He paid the price for his lack of care, because Bishop Hotham removed him from office that same year, on the grounds of his old age and infirmities, and appointed John de Crauden in his place. You will no doubt be pleased to know that the dismissed prior was not cast out of the community, but was allowed to remain in his old quarters until his death some seventeen years later. This did pose accommodation problems of course when John de Crauden was appointed prior that same year, but this was solved by the building of an extra study for John de Crauden and the erection of his now famed chapel, another part of Ely's superb fourteenth-century Decorated inheritance.

4 See F. R. Chapman, *Sacrist Rolls of Ely, 2 vols* (Cambridge, Cambridge University Press, 1908), part ii, Roll viii, p. 62.

As far as we can ascertain, the total debt owed by the community represented about three years' estate income, which had remained fairly constant at about £1,200 a year during this period. It seems that income from the shrine of St Etheldreda was not particularly impressive either, at about £50 per annum at this time.

We do have a valuable insight into the mind of Prior Crauden just after the collapse of the tower, because we can read the translation of his letter to the King, explaining what had happened and the difficulties the community faced. The letter says:

> May it please your Royal Highness to know that your church of Ely founded by your ancestors, on whose souls may God have mercy, has utterly collapsed to the ground within the past month together with the tower and breaking the bells. The church and we from the time of John of Fresingfield within the past year our Prior, who left his post of prior by reason of the intolerable load of debt, have been so unexpectedly burdened with various dues, that the largest part of our goods, for the debt to you of which we have already paid a great sum to your exchequer in the fortnight of the Purification of the Blessed Mary, remains still confiscated in your hands until the full payment of your same debt which we are albeit continually trying to raise. Thus the payment of this debt together with the repair of our, *or rather your* said church will be impossible for our times, unless with your wonted clemency your affection should have compassion upon us, and after overcoming your enemies, which issue may God hasten, should lay upon us a helping hand in the calm of the peace that follows. — May it please your most merciful clemency to excuse our lack of power in this behalf, *and regard us as unable to obey the tenour of your letter delivered to us recently by your messenger that we would look on you more liberally.*[5]

I rather like the hint of gentle blackmail implicit in his final sentence!

5 See T. D. Atkinson, *An Architectural History of the Benedictine Monastery of St Etheldreda at Ely* (Cambridge, Cambridge University Press, 1933), p. 175 [my italics].

The Cathedral in 1321

The plan view of the cathedral in 1321, before the community began to dig the foundations of the new Lady chapel, would have been a model of symmetry.

Opposite: The Lady chapel, east end

In the thirteenth century, the original Norman church, in plan the traditional cross shape, had been extended towards the west by the Galilee porch, and to the east by Bishop Northwold's fabulous six-bayed presbytery. This latter extra space was required to house more conveniently the relics of St Alban, St Etheldreda, and the three other Anglo-Saxon saints in their shrines, and the press of pilgrims visiting them. The transepts at the west end of the church still buttressed both sides of the west tower in comfortable symmetry, while Bishop Northwold's wooden spire still graced that tower's Norman summit. The central tower, supporting a clock and bells, stood at the crossing to mark the very centre of the community from which prayers and praise arose to the heavens. The former Lady chapel was at that time situated in the south presbytery aisle of the church. At first it almost adjoined the crossing and the monk's choir, and later, at the beginning of the fourteenth century, moved to a position nearer to the east end of that same aisle. The location of this chapel, and the difficulties of ensuring seclusion for the brothers, and privacy for worshippers in that chapel, many of them ladies, seem to have been the irritant in the oyster which ultimately gave rise to Ely's pearls—the Lady chapel, and thus the Octagon and the present choir.

If we examine the criticisms of visiting bishops contained in the Chapter Ordinances and Visitation Records[6] for the years leading up to the collapse, we can see a theme emerging. In the years 1300, 1307, and 1314, provisions appear which stress that the brothers are to refrain from '*superfluis confabulacionibus*' (idle gossip), especially it seems with '*suspectas et infamatas mulieres*'

6 *Ely Chapter Ordinances and Visitation Records, 1241-1515*, ed. S. J. A. Evans, Camden Miscellany, 16 (London, Royal Historical Society, 1940).

Sketch plan of the cathedral showing the general arrangement in 1321, featuring: (red) central stone tower, standing on four columns; (blue) monks' choir; (green) pulpitum or screen. The first (A) and second (B) positions of the Lady chapel are also indicated.

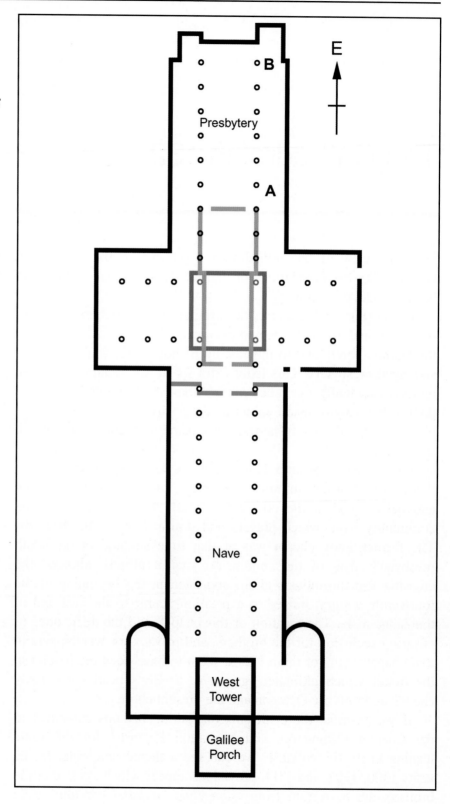

E

Presbytery

B

A

Nave

West Tower

Galilee Porch

(suspect and ill-famed women), who might be in and around the church. At one point, a partition is suggested to prevent monks from peeping from their choir into the former Lady chapel, and this may have prompted its move to the east end of the presbytery aisle. Other provisions stress that strangers are to be rigorously excluded from the choir, the cloister, and other parts of the monastery.

Without doubt however, Ely had lagged behind somewhat in the provision of a separate Lady chapel, and by all accounts it was the Marian enthusiasm of one brother, John of Wisbech the sub-sacrist, which provided the final impetus for the building operations to begin. Alan of Walsingham, the newly promoted sacrist, seems to have designed it to be a chapel to outshine all other chapels. One of the largest Lady chapels in Britain, it is one hundred feet long and forty-six feet wide, with the widest stone vaulted ceiling attempted up to that date. After all, up to 1321, Alan of Walsingham had been 'Keeper of the former Lady chapel', and knew the likely importance of the new chapel in attracting future pilgrims to the shrine of St Etheldreda. He also would have been acutely aware of the criticisms implicit in the strictures of the Visitations and the Ordinances, and the shortcomings of the rather cramped and overlooked Lady chapel in the south choir aisle.

We also know from the writings of the famous chronicler Thomas Walsingham (no relation), that in 1314 or so, Alan of Walsingham had assisted Edward II to adjudicate on the provenance of supposed relics of St Alban which had been kept under somewhat dubious circumstances here at Ely. The shrine of St Alban at Ely was at the furthest east end of the presbytery towards the north wall.

Despite the repeated requests of the St Albans community over the years, the relics had not been returned, and patience became exhausted. The monks of St Albans eventually retorted that the original, genuine relics had not been sent to Ely for safekeeping anyway, but had been secreted in St Albans' abbey all along.

The Ely relics of St Alban were kept in a sealed reliquary which Alan with his skill as a goldsmith was asked to open to enable the King to examine them.

Edward agreed that the relics at St Albans were the genuine ones, and the consequent loss of such prestigious relics to Ely would likely have been a serious blow to the shrine income here. Perhaps Alan thought it was time for a major uplift to the reputation of the sacred shrine of St Etheldreda and the Virgin

Mary. Up until 1321, it could have been said that the Ely community's adoration of their own holy virgin, Etheldreda, had obscured their need to pay sufficient respect to the Holy Virgin, and this was now to be remedied. The new sacrist, Alan, promoted to this very senior post in the monastery, was about to provide a chapel of which the community could be proud.

We now know of course that that pride came before a fall. A fall which nevertheless initiated one of the most important cathedral building campaigns of the fourteenth century, and which has left us such a wonderful Decorated inheritance.

Dramatis Personae in 1321

Bishop John de Hotham

The most nationally prominent member of the cast of our drama, Hotham was an outsider in Ely terms. His first contact with the community was in 1316 when he was appointed bishop. First mentions of him appear in connection with Piers Gaveston, Edward's first favourite. Hotham seems to have been adept at attaching himself to powerful friends, and at first he was known as a firm adherent of Gaveston. D. J. Stewart, our Victorian sacrist, clearly had a very jaundiced view of Hotham and said that he 'had a considerable share in most of the transactions which disgraced the reign of that feeble King'.[7] Hotham, a scion of an illustrious Yorkshire family (who as the 'de Houldhams', had come over from Normandy with William I), first rose to prominence as one of the King's clerks based in the York diocese. Edward I had been so often on campaign in the North against the Scots that a convenient power base had evolved in the city of York, and the beginnings of a vigorous 'civil service' had arisen from the need to administer England from York. The King also found it mightily useful to reduce his salary burdens by allowing the Church to pay his clerks 'in holy orders'. Hotham himself seems always to have been exceedingly rich, and for example in 1309 we find him appointed by the King as a tax gatherer in Yorkshire collecting a tax of one twenty-fifth on all moveable assets to provide for the wars in Scotland. In the same year he is loaning considerable sums of his own money to Earl Mortimer of Wigmore who was strapped for cash on his return to England after an assignment as Viceroy of Ireland. This association with Mortimer was to continue, mostly to Hotham's huge advantage, for all of Edward II's reign, and it was only ended when Mortimer was removed from power and executed

7 See D. J. Stewart, *On the Architectural History of Ely Cathedral* (London, J. Van Vorst, 1868), p. 83.

in 1330 after a 'coup' organised by Edward III at Nottingham to regain control of his kingdom.

Returning to Hotham's career, we find that because of Gaveston's demise he lost his appointment as 'Keeper of the Forests, North of the Trent', a very profitable sinecure, but almost immediately, in 1313, fell into the appointment as Prebend of Stillington, in the York diocese. From the scant information available it seems that Edward took advantage of a long-standing dispute between the Pope and the diocese over who should be appointed, and appointed Hotham while they were squabbling. It goes without saying that this prebendary was an extremely lucrative sinecure.

In 1315 and 1316 he was doing valuable administrative work in Ireland, and again in 1316, we see him joining 'the Middle Party'. Consisting mainly of clerics, this body sought to find a middle way between the high-handed activities of the monarch and the extreme remedies being proposed by the magnates of the realm, who felt that preferment was being given to entirely unsuitable people (mostly not to themselves). In the Middle Party we find Hotham and his close friend John Saleman, Bishop of Norwich, who until 1298 had been prior of Ely, and they conducted an embassy to Avignon to explain their aims and intentions to the Pope.

John Saleman was a member of the legendary family of Ely goldsmiths, the Salomans. They were the hereditary goldsmiths of Ely monastery, and Alan of Walsingham was also a member of that family. John was Alan's uncle and this may prove to be of significance to our story.

In short, John Saleman may have eased Hotham towards the Ely post, and when Hotham later required a sub-prior as a matter of some urgency, he may have felt inclined to help a Saloman in return. It is also significant, I think, that John de Fressingfield, who would have known John Saleman of Norwich well (they were both at Ely together until about 1298 when Saleman became Bishop of Norwich), proposed Hotham as the new Bishop of Ely and indeed supervised his election.

Hotham became Bishop of Ely in 1316, and by 1318 was also Lord Chancellor. John Saleman became Lord Chancellor in 1320.

In 1321, Hotham was forced to remove John de Fressingfield from his post as prior, because of the huge debts that had accumulated during Fressingfield's attempts to enlarge the monastery's estates. It is hinted strongly that the old prior had become unable to carry out his duties because of old age and his infirmities, but it might also be true that Hotham, a rich and successful man, could no longer bear to watch the deterioration of the community's position. In the chapter house, Fressingfield, 'surrounded by those that loved him', was removed from office, and at the same meeting, Alan of Walsingham was appointed sub-prior as a stopgap measure. Shortly after, John de Crauden, a senior monk at Ely, was appointed prior, and Alan became the sacrist.

Just a few weeks later came the planned start to the Lady chapel operations, and within the year, the unplanned catastrophe that set the fourteenth-century building programme in motion.

After the collapse, Hotham took responsibility for the refurbishment of the three bays that we now know as the choir, but sadly died before the completion of the new work. He died in 1337 and is buried most appropriately within the choir and just to the West of his close colleague John de Crauden, who is buried at his feet.

As F. R. Chapman points out in his book, *Sacrist Rolls of Ely*, Hotham moved in exalted circles and would have taken note of the new building developments and programmes at Westminster; he would also have been kept closely informed of new work at St Paul's where his nephew was a canon. Hotham was Lord Chancellor of England in the period 1318 to 1320 and again in 1328, and he was the Bishop of Ely who gave his manor and estate of 'Oldborne', together with six tenements, to become the Bishop of Ely's residence in London, i.e. Ely Place, Holborn.

Hotham can be summed up as an ambitious man, a successful civil servant and a man with huge influence in the establishment. One also gets the message from various sources that he 'was of little learning'. Nevertheless, Hotham was held in high esteem by the monastery at Ely for all the privileges and advantages he was able to obtain for the community, and when faced with a crisis they looked to him for protection. On one occasion when the Exchequer had made application to the monks for payment of a long outstanding debt, they wrote to Bishop Hotham to ask him to use his influence to obtain further time to pay. They said that 'they had rested under the shadow of his wings, they thanked him as their Good Shepherd, but now the sleeping dog is awakened by the Barons of the Exchequer'. History does not record whether this spectacularly mixed metaphor achieved its purpose.

Prior John de Crauden

John had been at Ely for many years when we first encounter him in the records in 1316 or so. He is listed as one of the senior monks involved in a committee of enquiry which was investigating the rights and wrongs of a dispute between the sub-prior and the tertius (third) prior, which had arisen during an absence of John de Fressingfield the prior. The sub-prior felt his junior had slighted his authority, but eventually they kissed and made up in obedience to the committee, and Fressingfield.

We have already seen that Prior Crauden obtained his office when de Fressingfield was removed in 1321, and he was faced with the immediate threat of the monastery's huge indebtedness, to among others, the King himself. Having seen his rather wily letter to the King, I often wonder if the King's response might have been to make some sort of 'voluntary contribution' to the works at Ely. Could just such a contribution have given rise to that slightly incredible story of the pot of coins found under mysterious circumstances in the Lady chapel foundations by the monk John of Wisbech? It was said that the accidental 'find' was so valuable that John was able to pay all the workmen's wages for a considerable time.

Idle speculation aside, Crauden seems to have earned the respect and admiration of all around him for his business acumen, his charm, and his piety. He may have taken to heart the advice of Bishop Orford who visited the monastery in 1307 and suggested that the then prior (John de Fressingfield) should aim to be 'loved rather than feared'. Crauden became a close confidante and friend of Queen Phillipa, who visited the monastery on many occasions, and eventually built the little suite of rooms called to this day 'The Queen's Apartments', for such visits.

Because the deposed prior was to continue living in his old rooms, Crauden asked Alan the sacrist to build his new timber first-floor study ('for his books when he had the leisure to look at them') and the adjoining stone chapel ('where he also carried on frequently through days and nights, his prayers and spiritual meditations').

Crauden was held in such high regard by his colleagues that he was elected by the convent unanimously as the new Bishop of Ely on the death of John de Hotham in 1337. Sadly, 'he failed of success' and Simon de Montacute was appointed instead.

He died in 1341 and is buried at the feet of Hotham just inside the present choir screen.

Alan of Walsingham

Alan is such a hero here at Ely, and as a result we could be for-given for adding to the 'halo' effect. We must therefore be careful to give credit only where we have good evidence, and at a distance of almost 650 years since his death, this will be quite difficult.

We know very little of Alan's early life, except that he was a member of the illustrious Ely family the Salomans, who were goldsmiths in the town.[8] His mother and father are named as Adam and Agnes of Walsingham.

The family had close links with the Church and the monastery and indeed had provided a prior in the twelfth century quite apart from holding hereditary posts as goldsmiths within the monastic community. As goldsmiths, the family were probably Ely's first bankers, in that other folk would ask them to store their gold and valuables in their strong rooms, while the Salomans would issue promissory notes which could be 'spent', much like modern bank-notes.

Alan, it seems, had already become a fully fledged goldsmith before entering the monastery, and we first find him engaged in that role to help Edward II gain access to the supposed relics of St Alban in the sealed reliquary. Later, at the time that John de Crauden was heading the committee to deal with the sub-prior's complaint, Alan does not appear in a list of senior monks, so perhaps we can deduce that he was still a very junior monk then. A little later we find he is *custos* or guardian of the Lady chapel, then situated in the presbytery south aisle.

Sudden and dramatic promotion came Alan's way when Hotham removed Fressingfield from the office of prior, and at the same chapter house meeting installed Alan as sub-prior. He was now the senior monk in the community and all would have to answer to him. This interregnum did not last long, however, and as soon as Crauden had been formally elected prior in 1321, Alan became the sacrist, a post he held for twenty years until the death of Crauden in 1341, when he himself was elected prior. The post of sacrist was pivotal to the successful functioning of the community, and in terms of precedence was third in line after the prior and sub-prior. The sacrist had many and varied duties which included supervising the provision of bread and wine of high quality for the sacraments, and in addition he oversaw legal matters concerning the estates of the monastery and was charged with collecting rents and debts. Without doubt, however, his responsibility for maintaining and repairing the convent's buildings was of the

8 See F. R. Chapman, *Sacrist Rolls of Ely*, Appendix C for further details.

greatest importance in terms of our story of the rebuilding of the centre of the cathedral. Alan's tenure of the post of sacrist is of course distinguished mostly by his efforts in transforming the great church itself from the wreck left by the collapse, and his provision of the Lady chapel, Prior Crauden's chapel, the new sacristy and the extension to the infirmary block, which initially he used as his own private quarters.

On the death of Bishop Montacute in 1345, Alan was unanimously elected by the community to succeed him as Bishop of Ely, but Pope Clement VI conferred the bishopric on Thomas de Lisle. Alan died in 1364 and is buried just to the west of the former monk's choir in the centre aisle of the nave. The somewhat battered grave slab, now missing its brasses, has a space at the foot of it where Alan's lengthy epitaph was placed. In a small sign of defiance to the Pope's ruling about Alan's election as bishop, the monks portrayed him wearing a mitre on the grave brass.

The Collapse of the Norman Crossing Tower in 1322

We know very little about Ely's original crossing tower. It was always referred to as 'Abbot Richard's tower', and we know that it stood on four massive pillars at the central crossing. It was built at the very beginning of the twelfth century and probably mostly finished before the nave was completed in 1130 or so. This tower contained several bells and a clock, and its four supporting pillars enclosed the western end of the monks' choir, the spiritual centre of the community. Many visitors ask how high the tower might have been, but there are no hints in the available material. One suggestion has been that the original tower may have been slightly higher than the west tower as completed at the end of the twelfth century. We may reasonably speculate that Alan designed the new tower to be as imposing in stature as the old tower it replaced, and the height of the new tower to the top of the Lantern is one hundred and seventy feet, or fifty-two metres.

Rather surprisingly, our best authority and the earliest account of the fall of the crossing tower is contained in a book first published in 1691, so not at first sight a contemporary account. The book is *Anglia Sacra* (The Diocese of Britain) by Henry Wharton. As quite a young man, Henry was appointed librarian and archivist at Lambeth Palace and was therefore very familiar with document 448 MSS, Lambeth, which is the original *Chronicle of the Abbots and Bishops of Ely* as compiled by anonymous monks of Ely in the twelfth to the sixteenth centuries. Wharton in fact edited these original records but stuck closely to the text, so I will do no more than quote and translate Wharton's and the chronicler's words which describe the circumstances of the collapse. These words are then almost certainly a contemporary account of the fall of the original tower.

Nam in nocte ante diem Festi Sanctae Erminildae, post matutinas in Capella S. Katerinae decantatas eo quod in choro propter imminentem ruinam illas decantare conventus non audebat, facta namque processione ad feretra in honore S. Erminildae, et conventu in dormitorium regrediente, vix paucis fratribus in lectulis suis ingressis, et ecce subito et repente ruit campanile super chorum cum tanto strepitu et fragore; veluti putabatur terrae motus fieri; neminem tamen laedens nec opprimens in ruina.

For in the night before the feast day of St Ermenilda, after matins in the chapel of St Catherine (sung there because the assembly did not dare to sing the service in the choir hard by because of its imminent ruin), they processed to the shrine of St Ermenilda, said a prayer, and then returned to their dormitory. Scarcely a few of the brothers had got into bed and behold suddenly all at once the bell tower fell with much crashing and banging—as though, it were thought, there had been an earthquake. Nevertheless, no one was injured or crushed in the ruins.

My translation from the original Latin gives us some clues as to the actual date of the fall of the tower. The feast day of St Ermenilda (Saxon name Ermengild) was, and still is, 13 February. The words 'night before', suggests the night of the 12–13 February because 'the night' in monk's terms extended from 6 p.m. on the twelfth to 6 a.m. on the thirteenth. The words 'after matins' give us a likely time of around 4.30 a.m., taking into account the extra prayer for St Ermenilda. One wonders at the trepidation of the monks as they briefly crossed under the unsafe tower to go to and from St Ermenilda's shrine situated at the east end of the presbytery. As far as I can ascertain there was no other route to the northeast corner of the presbytery where St Ermenilda's tomb was located, but by way of the old centre of the cathedral, perhaps via the door in the southern wall of the south transept (now blocked).

As to the reference to St Catherine's chapel, this was not of course the present St Catherine's chapel in the southwest transept, but the earlier chapel of that name which was sandwiched between the original chapter house and the south transept.

One extra note of explanation is required about the brothers getting back into bed at such a time. You may already have guessed that they were allowed a perfectly legal snooze between matins and preparations for 'Prime', the next service at 6 a.m.

Oh and by the way, it was a Saturday the thirteenth, and not Friday the thirteenth!

As you read the various sources of information you will find that no less than four dates are quoted for the collapse, the twelfth, the thirteenth, the twenty-first, and the twenty-second, all thank-

The blocked door in the southern wall of the south transept

fully in February. The twelfth seems the most popular, especially if the writer concerned has translated *nam in nocte ante diem* as 'the eve', and has omitted the all-important *post matutinas* 'after Matins', i.e. about 4 a.m.

In my view then, the tower fell at about 4.30 a.m. on the thirteenth of February, only very narrowly missing the column of monks returning to their dormitory.

I have not found any explanation for the last two dates but I note that Dean Stubbs, no less, quotes the twenty-second in his 1896 lectures (see bibliography).

The passage from *Anglia Sacra*, last sentence, also gives the tour-guide the answer to one of the most frequently asked questions about the collapse. No one was hurt or crushed by the tower's fall.

It is quite clear that the monks had been warned that the crossing tower was dangerously unstable, and for some time they had been preparing themselves for the fall, and for the effort of re-building the crossing. Whilst they were fulsome in their praise and admiration of St Etheldreda for protecting the holy shrines, and for preserving their own lives during the fall, they were clearly taken aback by extent of the damage, which was far worse than they had imagined possible.

Alan of Walsingham is portrayed as perplexed and over-whelmed and not knowing what to do or which way to turn. The monks' choir had been totally obliterated and smashed by the falling masonry and there was 'much dust'. The hole torn in the roof by the falling tower was perhaps in the region of seventy-one feet (twenty-two metres) in diameter, and the four arms of the church had been all but disconnected from each other. One small consolation slowly emerged as the rubble was cleared. The relics and bones of Ely's seven Anglo-Saxon benefactors buried in the north wall of the choir enclosure had survived unscathed, to be re-buried in the new north wall of the choir under the new Octagon in due course. These 'benefactors' were eminent Saxons who in the tenth century had endowed the newly refounded Benedictine monastery with lands and estates to guarantee its financial future. Six of them were eminent churchmen, including the famous Wulfstan, Archbishop of York, and one, a famous warrior, Brithnoth. As a result of their endowments they were all greatly revered at Ely.

Nevertheless, the task before the community seemed impossible, if only for the huge total of debts outstanding to among others, Edward II, King of England, who had already sequestered the monastery's assets in lieu of payment. Meanwhile, there was also the problem of how the Lady chapel project would be completed. The foundations for this work had been laid in 1321, the year before the collapse.

Anglia Sacra makes it plain, however that no time was lost in clearing the rubble and dust of the fall 'with alacrity', and before long we see Alan marking out eight new places for the columns that will support the new crossing tower, and making doubly sure that the new foundations are very sound.[9]

The account of the collapse often provokes the question from visitors—do we know why the tower collapsed? In answer we can only offer likely theories, of course. Professor Jacques Heyman explains the 'generation rule' which particularly applies to Norman crossing towers. If the crossing survives successfully without problems of serious settlement for at least twenty years, then it will likely last 500 years, or more, and its working life will be limited only by the failure of its fabric material, or some alteration to the soil mechanics beneath it.[10] Since our crossing tower had already survived 212 years or so, it seems likely that some alteration of the water table under the crossing had weakened the ground beneath. It is perhaps significant that the Lady chapel foundations were started in 1321, and this area of disturbed ground was only about twenty-five metres or so from the nearest corner of the crossing.

9 See Henry Warton, *Anglia Sacra* (Londini, 1691), p. 644.
10 See J. Heyman, *The Stone Skeleton: Structural Engineering of Masonry Architecture* (Cambridge, Cambridge University Press, 1995), p. 25.

Philip Dixon, the cathedral archaeologist, explains that the high water table under the central area of the cathedral seems always to have caused problems, even when the building was first under construction. He has seen evidence of ten-foot-deep trenches, dug in antiquity under the cathedral, in an attempt to stop water from underground springs pooling under the building. To see how springs burst forth from the adjoining strata of the lower clays and the thin lower greensand cap of the Isle of Ely, one only needs to walk across Ely City Golf Course, down the southern slope towards the station, where you can see a stream with small outcrops of lower greensand in its bed. How much wetter was the sub-soil in 1322?

Reconstruction

Document 448 of the Lambeth MSS and *Anglia Sacra* both confirm the salient dates of the construction of the new Octagon tower and the new campanile, the Lantern, suspended within it. The stone tower, an octagon in form, which stitches together the four damaged arms of the church, was mostly completed in six years up to 1328, while the complicated wooden structure within took no less than a further fourteen years to be finished. Even so, finishing touches were still being made into the early 1350s.

Opposite: The sacrist's arch. Alan of Walsingham built his headquarters here in 1325–1326.

The total cost is mentioned in the sacrist rolls as being £2,406 6s. 11d. The community itself furnished the major part of this sum, with about £200 or so coming from donations from friends and well-wishers. Alan's uncle John Saleman, Bishop of Norwich, donated some £15. The ordinary monks of the monastery made a very noble contribution by giving up their 'pittances' or pocket money for little luxuries like cakes and wine at Christmas and on other feast days. This sad state of affairs seems to have continued for several years of the rebuilding.

Shortly after the collapse, the remains of the four great pillars on which the old tower had stood had been cleared away very quickly together with large quantities of dust and rubble. Alan seems to have decided at this point that he would not use the very centre of the crossing ground to support his new tower, presumably on the grounds that it was too unstable to trust. He decided to shorten each of the four arms of the church by one bay at the centre of the church, and make a much wider crossing area. In effect he was moving the supports for his new tower outwards by one bay, or arch. He famously took the advice of 'someone who came up from London' and accordingly marked out eight places to be the new foundations for the eight pillars that would support the new octagonal stone tower. Of necessity, these eight locations were

Sketch plan of the cathedral to show the new general arrangement as at 1350, featuring: (red) new octagonal central tower; (blue) new monks' choir; (green) pulpitum or screen. N.B. The processional way originally provided in the fourteenth century between the Lady chapel and the presbytery was at a more acute angle than the year 2000 version. The original line is preserved in the low wall in front of the entrance to the washrooms and kitchen.

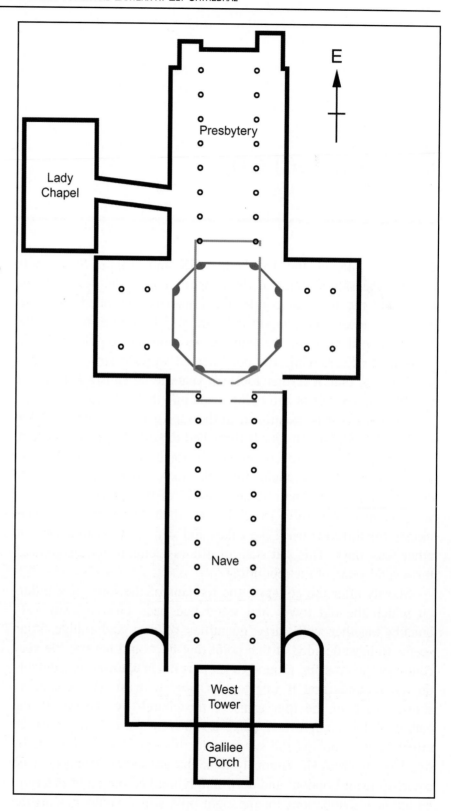

adjacent to the eight damaged piers that remained of the old structure, and Alan went to great lengths to ensure that the foundations of these old piers were adequately reinforced to take the new loads. We know that in Alan's time, when the numerology of buildings and churches was of great significance, the number eight always referred to 'redemption and renewal', and maybe Alan, who was essentially a practical man, allowed himself a wry smile when choosing to replace four pillars with eight, for it was clear that the new structure would have to span eight arches. Once he had decided to disregard the four old pillar sites, presumably in the belief that the ground beneath them could no longer be relied upon, the obvious solution was an octagon (or put another way, a square with four corners clipped), a form that fitted very well with the architectural fashions of the early fourteenth century. In addition he would have been aware that eight also represented 'eternity', and this surely was his overall intention—to portray our eternal life stretching away above us. We even see the portrait of Christ above us displaying his crucifixion wounds to remind us of our redemption.

Other forms could possibly have been used to consolidate the centre of the damaged cathedral, but none other could have combined function with economy, the true engineer's mantra. In my view, once the decision to avoid the centre of the crossing ground had been made, a resultant square tower would have been too large an area to roof successfully, whilst a circular form would no doubt have meant complicated geometry at each of the eight crossing arches. Even the octagonal tower, it seems, was thought to have some possible weaknesses, notably at the four shorter sides where four large windows span the four aisle arches. Alan seems to have forestalled future difficulties there, by providing elegant and unique flying buttresses at ninety degrees to each other, which in effect brace the structure against each of the four arms of the building. The sizeable pinnacle that stands sentinel immediately outside each of the four huge windows has been placed there to take directly the outward thrust of the raking shores which support the main weight of the Lantern. Each of those supports finds its feet in the masonry of the tower either side of those great windows, just where the buttresses adjoin the tower.

In considering these complicated support structures, it seems to me that further evidence of Alan's abilities emerges. Alan would have been used to the convention that roofs of large buildings like the nave and the presbytery needed to be high and steep in order to reduce the sideways thrust at the parapet of the walls. When

A sketch to show how the Lantern is suspended within the Octagon tower. Only the western half is shown for clarity. Red denotes the framework of the Lantern, i.e. the great oaks, green denotes the 'raking shores' inside the tower, and yellow represents the stone buttressing to the exterior pinnacles.

roofing the Octagon tower, he was faced with considerable problems if he intended to use the top of the tower to support his new roof because it might not be strong enough to cope with the outward thrust. My thought is then, when we look at the supporting beams of the Lantern in section, are we not looking at the real 'roof line' which Alan has ingeniously placed lower within the hollow tower, where it can be successfully braced by the huge mass of the nave, the choir and presbytery, and the two main transepts?

One of the four sets of opposing flying buttresses at the shorter sides of the Octagon. This is the southwest corner between the nave and the south transept. The base of the buttress pillar intrudes on the ancient doors to the vestry and the monks' door.

Because the eight spaces to be bridged by the new tower were unequal in width, the resultant octagon could not be equilateral. It has four longer sides to bridge the nave, choir, and the north and south transepts and four shorter sides to bridge the interposing side aisles of the four arms of the church.

We are told that Alan consulted his masons and carpenters before beginning the tower, but that it was his genius that evolved the finished design that we see above us. He certainly had collected together a fine team of masons and carpenters. There was John of Ramsey to lead the masons and, somewhat later in the story,

William Hurley, a carpenter of considerable reputation already, who had done great work for some of the highest in the land. It is Hurley who is credited with the highly original design of the Octagon roof and the Lantern, which incorporates in a very novel way earlier technology developed to build huge chimneys on mediaeval kitchens.[11] The new developments portrayed in the Octagon and Lantern would eventually lead to hammer-beam roofs, which grace so many later mediaeval buildings, but even so the techniques involved in building the Lantern were from traditional carpentry practice. Mortise and tenon joints fix the main components of the Lantern framework together (i.e. one beam has a slot cut in it to accommodate a tongue at the end of the beam to be joined to it; a tapered oak peg is driven through both elements to ensure a tight and secure joint). Lapped dovetail joints also feature in the construction of the fans of flooring joists (a dovetail-shaped recess is cut into the top surface of a substantial beam to enable a dovetail-shaped tongue on a lesser beam to be secured into it; once again secured by an oak peg, this joint resists both inward and outward movement). No other fixings apart from traditional carpenters' joints appear to have been used in the original construction by Hurley.

Thus it was decided to roof the hollow stone tower with a wooden roof, and to suspend a wooden Lantern in the centre to illuminate the crossing with natural light. The bells would be housed in a campanile built on top of the Lantern. When we look up into the glorious, soaring, vaulted ceiling, it is hard to convince ourselves that it is entirely made of wood. A combination of curved English oak ribs, and pine planks imported from the Baltic, create a wonderful Decorated, star-shaped extravaganza. The sacrist's rolls for 1323–1324 have entries for 'Rigold' boards obtained from Riga in Latvia and imported via the port of Lynn, and these presumably were employed in the lower vaulting of the roof. Similarly the rolls for 1334–1335 show that 'estrich' boards were purchased for the upper vaults. In researching the origin of this wood, I came across its optional mediaeval name of 'ostrich' wood, a white straight-grained pine wood, used to line tables on which designs could be drawn. It seems that this wood was originally sourced from 'Osterriech' or Austria, via Germany, but in the fourteenth century probably came from the Baltic. Most remarkably, both types of softwood boards have survived in their original positions[12] for well over six hundred years.

Alan was clearly building to the glory of God, but also to the

11 See John Fletcher, 'Medieval Timberwork at Ely', in *Medieval Art and Architecture at Ely Cathedral: The British Archaeological Association Conference Transactions for the Year 1976*, ed. Nicola Coldstream and Peter Draper ([London], British Archaeological Association, 1979), p. 63.

12 Ibid., p. 65.

honour of St Etheldreda whose shrine it was intended to be. Dean Stubbs, who delivered lectures on the Octagon and Alan of Walsingham in 1896 at Cambridge, was fond of describing it as the saintly crown of Etheldreda, and strangely, many visitors use the adjective 'jewel-like' to describe the Octagon and Lantern. Alan was after all a fully-fledged goldsmith and his designs might naturally have strayed towards the familiar shapes of precious objects.

Is there really any evidence of such wonderful co-operation and synchronicity between Alan and the masons and carpenters who built our great treasure? The overwhelming beauty of the design of the Octagon suggests strongly that Alan was one of the first English architects of ability, but in addition we can undoubtedly see him as one of the first truly great project engineers, who was able to grasp quickly the need for considerable co-ordination. In very short order:

- Bridges and causeways were strengthened and repaired to take the expected traffic of stone, timber, rushes etc.
- His servants were dispatched almost immediately after the collapse, to find the huge tree trunks of sufficient length and girth to complete the Lantern, a design he must already have been well on the way to finalising many years before its eventual completion. As we know they purchased eight suitable trees and twelve others for the sum of nine pounds from the nuns of Chicksands Priory. If, as I think entirely possible, those same huge trees were to provide the vertical framework of the Lantern in 1335, then Alan must have planned to have somewhere in the region of thirteen or fourteen years for the oaks to shrink and season somewhat, but not to have become too difficult to work in that time. In that timespan the oaks would I understand have lost about half their original weight through drying out, but would have gained enormously in strength.
- Carts were specially strengthened with wrought-iron reinforcements to enable the huge oak trees to be transported from Chicksands to the Great Ouse and thence to Ely by barge.
- Some of the iconography of the Octagon and Lantern must already have been clear in his mind from the inception of the project, because the scenes from Etheldreda's life and miracles were swiftly ordered to be carved to enable them to be inserted as the stonework of the tower began to rise.
- Close attention to detail ensured co-operation between stonemasons and carpenters. Slots were designed into each corner of

the stone tower to take vertical wooden beams as a 'first fixing' for the wooden vaulting and the framework which would form the floor of the roof space.

- We are told that Alan asked the masons to leave their complex scaffolding in place when they had finished the stonework up to the rim of the stone tower, so that the carpenters could use it to begin to erect the elaborate support framework for the new campanile, the Lantern, which was to be suspended in the centre of the hollow stone Octagon.

- In the early days of the project, Alan sent a boy down to Essex to seek out a specialist crane builder, a certain Thomas Carpenter of Newport. He was found with some difficulty, and eventually came to Ely to build a crane for the agreed price of 6s. 8d. (thirty-three pence in today's currency). His travelling expenses were 2s. (ten pence). We surmise that during the erection of the Lantern and the roof, Thomas's crane would have been placed in turn on the top of the eight stairwells on the rim of the stone tower. These stairwells had flat tops throughout much of the Octagon's history, only acquiring their pinnacles in the nineteenth-century Scott restoration, in Dean Merivale's time.

In our study of the Octagon and Lantern we have now reached a crucial stage, and we are seriously handicapped almost immediately by the absence of all of the sacrist's rolls or expenditure records for the eight years between 1326 to 1334. We know from *Anglia Sacra* that the hollow stone tower was said to be finished in 1328, but other writers have speculated that the stonework was not finished completely but only up to the stage that the carpenter's work could be commenced. Others have suggested that there was a bit of a lull in operations, perhaps because of a lack of funds. (We will discuss this apparent pause a little later in the saga.)

Another drawback is that the two reverend gentlemen (Stewart and Chapman) who have assisted our efforts so far, begin to disagree about the order of service. If that was not enough, an extremely eminent expert on mediaeval carpentry, Cecil Hewett, sheds little real light on the most important elements of the Lantern and its method of construction, concentrating mostly on the elegant vaulting and the floor of the roof space of the Octagon itself.

Although somewhat altered in structure and details by two major restorations, the new crossing tower can be seen to be comprised of three main elements.

First of all, there is the hollow stone Octagon tower that was built to stitch together the four arms of the church after the collapse. It rose through the hole in the roof created by the collapse, and in diameter approximates to the size of that hole, i.e. seventy-one feet or almost twenty-two metres. It has four long sides to bridge the nave, the east end, and the transepts and alternately, four short sides to bridge the aisle arches.

The second element is the wooden Lantern, an equilateral octagon, with an internal diameter of about thirty feet or nine metres or so, which is propped inside the stone Octagon on sixteen major 'raking shores'. These 'shores' are huge oak beams at an angle of about sixty degrees. They extend from each corner of the Lantern from a point just above the level of the large, musical angels' heads, down either side of the eight major openings in the stone tower, which intrude into the wooden, star-shaped, vaulted ceiling (see page 30). Ingeniously, the Lantern itself is turned twenty-two and a half degrees in relation to the stone Octagon to present its eight points to the midpoints of the sides of the stone Octagon. Eight enormous oak trees, standing vertically, form the corners of the Lantern, and extend from the internal opening in the dome to the top of the turrets on the very top of the whole structure, a total height of sixty-three feet or twenty metres. I think that these must have been the trees that Alan asked his men to find in 1323, simply because he needed to be certain for the sake of his final design that such trees could be obtained. In my view, it is significant that they were purchased from the nuns at 'Chikkisands' (Chicksands) Priory as growing trees, and it may be that the timber purchased in the local markets could not approach the dimensions required.

The third element is the glorious wooden gilded vaulting, which has a dual purpose. In the first instance it provides a 'Decorated' cover for the rather stark, straight, raking shores which support the Lantern, and secondly the vaulting provides the third side of the triangular supports for the floor of the roof space, and horizontal location for the Lantern itself. The scattered and profuse carpenters' marks on some of the beams of the floor suggest strongly that those elegant 'fans' of flooring joists which radiate from the corners of the tower were probably shaped, jointed, and assembled within a 'pattern' marked out on the ground. When complete, they were then numbered, disassembled, and re-erected in their final positions at height. A remarkable feature of this flooring is that it comprises many different and nonstandard components in its graceful whole and precise reconstruction at height would have been essential.

It would be less than even-handed at this point to omit to mention that in the past much serious argument has revolved around the extent to which the Lantern is supported (a) by the sixteen raking shores and (b) the elegant wooden vaulting which rises to the sill on which the eight oak trees stand. As late as 2004, a visitor to the Octagon told me that he had just attended a conference in Kalamazoo, Michigan, at which such considerations had been discussed. In particular, and years before, the cathedral's own consulting engineer, Professor Jacques Heyman, and E. C. Wade of F. J. Samuely and Partners had set forth their calculations in a paper to the Institution of Civil Engineers in 1985.[13] My first and overwhelming difficulty is that my schoolboy maths do not run to understanding their calculations, and so I am thrown back on my own more empirical and simplistic judgement. As my reading has progressed I've formed the opinion that above all, Essex, the eighteenth-century architect who probably saved the Octagon from a potential disaster (we will discuss this later) seems to have grasped the fact that the sixteen raking shores were the most important element of support and went so far as to duplicate their effect with extra shores placed above the original ones. Not only that, but he seems to have been prepared to change, and in some ways compromise, the integrity of the structure of the vaulting and its triangular components of floor joists, curved ribs, and Octagon wall. Finally, if the elegant vaulting structure had been struggling under significant loads all these years (in particular when eight of the raking shores were crumbling at their bases in the eighteenth century, on the northern and eastern sides of the Octagon), would the slender oak ribs, and the even flimsier softwood boarding between them, be in such relatively untouched, undistorted, good shape?[14] Essex did report during his restoration work however, that when his workmen had been able to inspect the ends of the sixteen main supports, they found that the ends of seven or eight of the timbers were mostly decayed, and he said that 'the whole weight of the Lantern had rested long on the ribs that appeared outwardly'. Once again, the Octagon seems to provide more questions than hard and fast answers. My own summary would be that the raking shores provide the essential support for the Lantern, while the vaulting provides location for the base of the Lantern, support for the floor of the roof space, and the required Decorated screen for the somewhat stark raking shores.

13 E. C. Wade and J. Heyman, 'The Timber Octagon of Ely Cathedral', *Institution of Civil Engineers (Great Britain) Proceedings. Part I*, 78 (Dec. 1985), pp 1421–1436 (Paper No, P8895).

14 See John Fletcher, 'Medieval Timberwork at Ely', p. 65.

The sequence of the sacrist's rolls resumes after the eight-year hiatus with the roll for the year Michaelmas 1334 to Michaelmas 1335, and its contents have caused the differences between Stewart and Chapman. The roll firstly gives details of the painting of the internal vaulting of the new tower with red lead, and Chapman says that of necessity the heavy carpentry work of building the Lantern itself must already have been completed by then, or the vaulting itself could not have been built, and there would be no support for the roof at that stage.

Stewart, on the other hand, assumed that it was in this year that the great posts of the Lantern were raised because the entry in the roll says, 'eight carpenters were boarded at the Abbot's expense' —*pro exaltatione magnarum postium in novo choro*—'for the raising of the great posts in the new choir'. Chapman tries to reconcile the position by saying that perhaps the roll refers to great posts other than the angle posts of the Lantern, perhaps in the ritual choir somewhere, but it is very difficult to see where such posts would be employed other than in the Lantern proper. To my mind, *postium* means a vertical post, and the only vertical posts in the new choir are the eight angle posts of the Lantern itself. All the other woodwork could only be said to be framing, vaulting or flooring. (I am excluding the short vertical posts inserted in the stonework of the tower, because they would have been installed at an early stage, as part of the initial framing.) One extra piece of evidence to take into account is that the name of William Hurley, the famous master carpenter, appears in this sacrist roll for the first time, and with a considerable salary of £8 marked against his name for that year. Maddeningly, because of the eight-year gap in the sacrist's rolls between 1326 and 1334, this does not enable us to say with confidence when he first came to Ely to give Alan the benefit of his advanced carpentry techniques.

We do know, however, that the eight great angle posts of the Lantern itself were apparently erected in two separate linear parts, and all of the most important commentaries on the building process (Stewart, Chapman or indeed Hewett) betray that they were not aware of that fact.

The lower part of each post is some twenty feet long and extends from the internal opening in the dome to the present roof line just below the base of the Lantern windows. Enormous mortise and tenon joints just above the present roof line join both sections of each post. The scant evidence we have may suggest then that these lower parts of the structure were already in place in

1334. 'The dome' (i.e. the wooden roof on the roof space with its central octagon-shaped orifice, waiting for the upper Lantern to be erected) was already complete, with the lower part of the Lantern 'cylinder' standing on its huge raking shores, which were hidden behind the vaulting that was now ready for painting with undercoat in 1334–1335. In my view, one explanation of the apparent discrepancies is that the final forty-three feet of each of the great posts forming the sides of the visible Lantern were the 'great posts', which took William de Houk and his eight carpenters nine weeks to erect in the period Michaelmas 1334 to Michaelmas 1335. As we have already seen, the rolls give us details of the lodging expenses of these men for this period, met by the Abbot.

There is another enigma around the 'great posts' which is difficult to explain. Three of the lower twenty-foot sections are divided vertically in half and Hewett offers the solution that the Lantern was perhaps erected in three separate sections of one half, and two quarters. This would only seem to be possible if that stage of construction only involved the lower portion of the Lantern 'cylinder'. Even if this was the case, Thomas Carpenter and his crane must have strained mightily to erect such a huge and weighty structure. Perhaps the masons' scaffolding was substantial enough to provide the support needed at this critical stage to facilitate the erection of the lower Lantern cylinder in stages.

Before we leave our consideration of the Lantern and its construction, we need to address another discrepancy that has crept into the literature, and which has become so widespread that there is a need to illuminate the truth quite literally. It concerns a drawing made by Cecil Hewett[15] of the framing of the Lantern that quite clearly displays the sixteen raking shores as having a markedly curved profile.

Firstly however, I need to explain that William Hurley and his carpenters labelled each of the corners of the stone Octagon in a series A to H, starting with A on your immediate left as you enter the Octagon roof space from the stairway from the north transept. The identifying letters were cut into the beams with chisels, and can be seen at various points on the joists of the floor of the roof space.

If your guide shines a torch down the length of the great raking shore to your left as you enter the roof space (corner 'A'), you will see immediately that the enormous balk of timber that originally carried one sixteenth of the weight of the Lantern, is arrow straight. I have examined all sixteen of the raking shores and only

15 See Cecil A. Hewett, *English Cathedral and Monastic Carpentry* (Chichester, Phillimore, 1985), p. 120.

two or three seem to fail the 'intended straightness' test. A couple of them, at corners F and G are gently 'S shaped', while one of the shores at D is very curved in the way that Hewett suggests for all the shores. For some unaccountable reason, Hewett drew all the shores as having a gentle curve down to their bases in the stonework of the Octagon tower. This error has been faithfully reproduced in the many subsequent publications that have used his drawing to illustrate the structure. We have the assurances of the two men responsible for both of the main restorations of the Octagon, and indeed the assurance of Hewett himself, that the raking shores are the originals as placed there by William Hurley.

The next roll we have for the year Michaelmas 1336 to Michaelmas 1337 deals with the painting of the lower vault in its final colours of dark green, stone, red and gold, and we know from the wages record that William Shanks was the painter engaged. An entry that records the cost of a 'stout rope to let down the painter' suggests that William painted the lower vault 'continental style', dangling from a rope suspended from the top of the vault somehow. His precarious perch might explain the comments of the Victorian restorers that they could only find evidence of hurried and hasty work. The Reverend Stewart, who would have been able to inspect the mediaeval painting before it was obscured by Thomas Gambier Parry, the Victorian restorer, describes Shanks's work as 'rude daubing'. We know that William was provided with stencils of vellum to enable him to reproduce the required designs.

We are fortunate to have a description of the traces of mediaeval painting still visible on the lower vault at the time of the nineteenth-century restoration. A guidebook from 1880 says:

> ...the pattern was a series of quatrefoils, painted in stone colour on the wood, outlined black, and filled with green. The bosses of the upper Lantern, which are not carved, had been evidently painted and gilt, but the patterns of foliage were rough and too much injured to afford any distinct composition. The small amount of colouring that remained on some of the mouldings of the Octagon was principally of a bright red, but only in small patches, the groundwork having peeled off and the colour with it.

A goldsmith called Ralph 'le goldbetr', was given golden florins by Alan the sacrist and it was his task to beat out those coins into sheets of gold leaf to gild the wooden fan vaults. I read elsewhere[16] that foreign gold coins or florins were commonly used for this process at this time because English gold coins were quite rare before about 1344. The florin would be placed between sheets of

16 See *English Medieval Industries*, ed. J. Blair & N. Ramsay (London, Hambledon Press, 1991), p. 131, and footnote 104.

vellum and beaten out with hammers in what can only be described as a mind-numbingly tedious process. Each florin would yield as many as one hundred sheets of fine gold leaf about three and a half inches square.

By 1340 the roof of the campanile was completed, and the central carved boss, which portrays Christ displaying his crucifixion wounds, was placed centrally in the upper vault. This carving, completed by John of Burwell for the princely sum of 2s. (ten pence), and 'his meals at the Abbot's table', provides the summit of Alan's portrayal of our eternal life beckoning to us from the heavens. The promise of redemption seems implicit in the figure of Christ displaying his crucifixion wounds.

In that same year, William Brampton glazed some of the Lantern's upper storey with stained glass, and wood turners were engaged to carve the remaining bosses in the upper vaults. The Lantern windows that were not immediately glazed were apparently covered by *canvasii*, which was specially purchased from 'Lenn' (Lynn).

Additionally, the sacrist rolls tell us that in the year 1339–1340 the Lantern was roofed in lead by Simon the plumber, at a cost of £43. The considerable sum involved would seem to suggest that it was comprehensively covered in lead, much as it is now.

Finally, Master John of Gloucester, whose surname is expressed as 'Belleyetere' or literally 'bellcaster', completed the Octagon and Lantern in 1342 with the provision of the bells for the campanile. The entries in the rolls seem to confuse the costs of bells in the 'great campanile', i.e. the west tower, with those of the Lantern, but I take it that at least four bells, and maybe six, were provided for the central campanile in the Lantern.

A summary of the various stages of erection of the Octagon and Lantern would seem, conjecturally, to be as follows:

- Clearance of rubble and the establishing of eight solid foundations for the columns to support the hollow, octagonal, tower. The masonry of the tower incorporates purpose-built slots at each corner to house vertical beams strained back to the walls with stone hooks and horizontal beams. The masons' scaffolding is left in place once the stone tower is completed to a suitable stage for the carpenters to start work to erect the floor of the roof space. This stage reached by c.1328.
- 'Fans' of flooring joists fan out from those beams in the wall slots to the central eight-sided collar on which the Lantern

appears to stand. The decorative wooden vaulting of the lower vault completes the third side of support for the floor of the roof space.

- The huge raking shores to support the Lantern are inserted next and half-jointed to the floor construction.
- The twenty-foot-long bases of the great oaks are lifted next and placed on the ends of the raking shores and strained apart by the lower framing of the Lantern 'cylinder'. Again the masons' scaffolding would have proved essential to provide support while this process was under way. The roof, which is supported by the stone tower and the tops of the eight twenty-foot-long bases, is built next. This stage reached by *c.*1334, and the unique 'gothic dome' could be said to be complete.
- The period 1334–1335 sees the erection of the 'great posts above the choir'.
- Erection of the upper Lantern framework, the original wooden flying buttresses providing triangular support and resistance to the force of the wind in such an exposed position. This stage reached by 1339–1340.

Some have argued that the stonework of the Octagon was never really finished at that stage, and as we have already seen, if Alan intended the tower to be crowned with pinnacles, they were not destined to be provided until the Victorian restoration under Sir George Gilbert Scott in the nineteenth century.

In this last period of the original building work there are considerable purchases of specially finished stone that may relate to the elaborate carvings of the entablature round the top of the stone tower, and of the balustrade itself. For example stone called 'Kings table' is thought to refer to the ball flower frieze which adorns the tower just below the balustrade. One authority tells us that this frieze closely resembles the decoration on the King's throne at Westminster, hence 'King's table'.

One tiny piece of evidence which may suggest that the stone work of the tower may still have been rising in the final stages of completion, is that the lancet windows in the top storey of the stone tower (in batches of six and three in the long and short sides of the Octagon) are said to have some of the earliest of 'Perpendicular' features by no less an authority than J. H. Harvey.[17] He suggests that the continuance upwards of the stone mullions of the lancet windows until they meet the lintel above is very early evidence of development of the new Perpendicular style.

17 See John H. Harvey, *Henry Yevele c.1320 to 1400: The Life of an English Architect* (London, Batsford, 1944), p. 7.

Some Inferences and Conjectures

With regard to the last stage of the building of the stone tower, a chance conversation with the cathedral's own archaeologist, Philip Dixon, provided a new and exciting direction for my thoughts on the course of the final stage of building of the stonework, and perhaps an alternative possibility for Alan's original intentions for the final exterior design of the Octagon and Lantern. Philip pointed to sixteen stone corbels, installed in the walls of the tower either side of the eight corners and set somewhat lower in the fabric than the *oculi*, or round windows. These corbels seem to be part of the original fabric, but have no apparent usefulness to the present structure. Moreover, in most cases the stone of the corbels is sharp and unworn. I had always assumed that these corbels were part of a defunct mechanism for holding back the original timberwork into the slots in the corners of the stone tower.

Philip's suggestion is that these corbels may be part of an original design for a steeple of some kind, perhaps on the lines of the octagonal chapel at Aachen (Aix La Chappelle) built to house the relics of Charlemagne. As built in the thirteenth century this stone octagon at Aachen was surmounted by a small roof supporting a lantern with a steeple atop. Alan would undoubtedly have seen versions of the design, and could even have visited Aachen itself.

There are some features we can pinpoint on the present fabric which would be explained by a revision of the final design just before the Lantern itself was erected with that steeple. There are other reasons and factors too, which may help to explain the change of intention.

- We have already seen that the builders of the fourteenth-century work at Ely were intent, under Alan's guidance, to pick up on design features in the Romanesque and Early English parts of

The two 'unused' stone corbels just below the pair of round windows at each corner of the stone tower

the fabric, and modify them to suit their Decorated style. The examples we have already seen are the pillars bisecting the arches on the southwest transept and the niches in the Lady chapel and the Octagon.

- Alan also reproduces *oculi* that he saw just below the old parapet line of the Norman work on the west tower, and faithfully inserts them just below the parapet line of the north and south walls of the Lady chapel in similar fashion. In addition, he creates a particular formation with the *oculi* and the pointed tops of the Lady chapel windows, and this formation is itself an echo of an equivalent Romanesque design on the southwest transept. If we now look at the walls of the Octagon, from say the vantage point of the doorway from the north transept staircase, we can see the same formation of *oculi* and window tops, just below the string-course at the base of the lancet windows. Was this string-course (shown in red) intended to be the original parapet of the stone tower? It is even provided with pinnacles.

- Accepting this to be so for a moment, it also seems clear that a parapet on this line would not be entirely suitable or strong enough to take much side thrust from a heavy roof supporting a lantern and steeple, if all the weight was held at the height of the mystery corbels.

- A spire would however have been stylistically consistent with the pinnacles on the north and south transepts, and indeed North-wold's spire, which still topped the west tower. Our next-door

Above left: Southwest transept, east wall, Romanesque/transition style (twelfth century)

Above right: Lady chapel, north wall, Decorated style (fourteenth century)

Left: First conjectural parapet line (1328) in red. The green shading indicates the parapet line in the 1350s. The twelve pinnacles and the top of the balustrade date from the 1870s.

neighbour, St Mary's, also acquired its spire in the first quarter of the fourteenth century.

- There is some slight evidence to suggest a change of design at the point where the nave roof joins the Octagon tower. Seen from inside the tower, a pointed arch in the stonework at the ridge of the roof seems to have a rounded arch superimposed on it.

- If William Hurley only arrived on the scene in 1334 or so, bringing with him the techniques to enable the Lantern to be supported by its raking shores at a much lower level in the fabric, did this input of new technology initiate and make possible the changes which resulted in the present design? Because of the missing sacrist rolls we cannot establish exactly when Hurley enters the picture with his revolutionary technology.

- We have already seen that the final stages of the stonework necessitated heavy purchases of special and decorative stone, perhaps to build the extra stage of the tower, from the string-course below the lancet windows, up to present roof line and balustrade.
- The possible later date of completion of the stonework would also explain the appearance of elements of Perpendicular in the mullions of the lancet widows. I believe the superintending master mason was by now John Attegrene, who seems to have been a local, who had become the master mason sometime during the years when the sacrist rolls are missing. John would no doubt have wished to use the latest trends.

We will, of course, never know if our speculation has been useful in unravelling the mystery of the apparent hiatus in building operations, but it would go some way to explaining the 'pause' that some observers have detected, around the time the first phase of the stonework was completed in 1328. If we accept for a moment that Hurley's arrival in 1334 (or earlier), sparked major changes to the design of the wooden centre of the tower, the revised building schedule would (conjecturally, of course) be:

- Completion of stonework to the string-course above the *oculi* by 1328.
- Construction of the floor of present roof space supported by the wooden fan vaulting (using the mason's scaffolding on the inside of the tower).
- 1334 or perhaps before, input of Hurley's expertise to redesign the Lantern supports.
- Erection of the raking shores, half-jointed to the floor beams.
- Erection of the lower twenty-foot-long portions of the great oaks and the framing of the lower Lantern.
- Raising of the tower's stonework to present balustrade level, and completion of the roof.
- Raising the forty-three-foot-long sections of the oaks in 1334 or 1335 to form the visible Lantern.
- The remainder of the programme as previously described.

Dedication

In 1342, in a ceremony that underlined the importance of the influential community at Ely, Edward III, his wife Queen Phillipa, and their son Edward, the Black Prince, were present at the dedication of the new ritual choir under the glorious new Octagon and the first three refurbished bays of the eastern arm of the church.

Prior John de Crauden had died in 1341, just before the final completion of the Octagon and Lantern. No doubt however, he would have already had many opportunities to show his close friend and confidante, Queen Phillipa, progress on the prestigious new buildings that Alan had designed and built in the twenty years or so since he had been appointed sacrist. Alan had in effect transformed the community. Apart from the Octagon and Hotham's refurbished choir arches, the vast new Lady chapel with its sumptuous carvings and its uniquely extensive frieze of the life and legends of the Virgin Mary was nearing its completion. Fronting onto Stepil Row (now High Street) there was the new headquarters of the sacrist's department with its gatehouse and special premises for the goldsmiths' workshops. To the south, the infirmary had acquired a new large chamber, built by Alan initially for his own use as sacrist but later to serve as a convenient lodging house for close relatives who visited the monastery to see brothers and sons in the community.

Almost certainly, however, John would have been proudest of the new chapel and adjoining study that Alan had designed and built for him shortly after John had been appointed prior.

The Octagon and Lantern
in the Years 1342 to Date

When we approach Ely from across the fens, especially after dusk, and we see the Octagon and Lantern floodlit against the sky, we should perhaps reflect for a moment and offer thanks for their almost miraculous survival for over 666 years.

For many years after their completion and indeed through the troubled years of the Reformation and later the English civil wars, there is no hint of any major programme of repairs to the Octagon and Lantern. Indeed in both periods there were threats to the structure of the cathedral itself. At the time of the Reformation many other religious foundations saw their buildings plundered and dismantled to enrich their new owners, but fortunately Ely was sheltered from such depredations by the influence of Bishop Goodrich, a close supporter of King Henry VIII. Goodrich was successful in convincing the King that Ely Cathedral should continue to house his 'new foundation' under the new dispensation, and was also able to preserve most of the monastic buildings to house the priests who would officiate under the revised doctrines.

The years of the Commonwealth saw an even narrower escape for the venerable structure. After the imprisonment of Bishop Matthew Wren, and severe modification of the style of worship, proposals were drawn up to demolish and sell the fabric to provide funds for widows and children of Parliamentarian casualties, and it seems that only confusion and inertia allowed the cathedral to survive. Doubts crept in that the costs of demolition would make the process uneconomic.

As later surveys showed, any repairs made between completion and the late 1750s were slight and ineffective, and when our old friend Thomas Fuller wrote his *Worthies of Britain*, a travelogue of remarkable sights which was published posthumously in 1662, but probably written somewhat earlier, he said of the Lantern:

Opposite: The west tower and the southwest transept from the southeast

The Lantern at night, floodlit from within the Octagon

When the bells ring, the wood-work thereof shaketh and gapeth, (no defect but perfection of structure) and exactly chocketh into the joynts again, for that it may pass for the lively embleme of the sincere Christian, who, though he has motum trepidationis, of fear and trembling, stands firmly fixt on the basis of a true faith.

It may be that that book had a profound effect when it reached Ely because very shortly after it was published the bells were removed from the Lantern and not replaced.

Only thirty years or so after the removal of the bells, a catastrophic collapse of the west side of the north transept in 1699 shook the Dean and Chapter out of any complacency that had crept in about the overall condition of the cathedral. Having taken the enlightened decision to restore carefully the north transept to its former style and glory in almost every detail, Dean Lambe and his canons went on to order a detailed survey of the whole building in 1703. Although that report is now lost it seems to have thrown up a great many defects in the state of the Lantern, and it is therefore most surprising that instead of a major restoration program, the Dean and Chapter authorised repairs costing only £40. The repairs ordered were fairly minor involving replacement of some lead and replacing some timbers that had rotted with 'timber of the same scantling'. Even worse, the original roof was not performing well and the Lantern seems to have been deteriorating fast. Again only minor repairs seem to have been made and it was not until the Cambridge architect James Essex examined the whole cathedral in 1757 that alarm bells really rang. Essex discovered very quickly that there were two priorities if he was to avoid some major collapses. The roof of the presbytery had 'racked' (i.e. had sagged eastwards in the absence of effective tie bars), and was now leaning heavily towards the east, pressing on the east wall of the cathedral with such persistent force that the wall was as much as two feet (sixty centimetres) out of the perpendicular at its gable peak. The report on the Lantern was so dramatic that it will be best to let it speak for itself:

> The prodigious quantity of Timber and Lead of which it is composed, was at first supported by sixteen pieces of timber only, of which number seven or eight are now rotten and unfit for supports, so that the whole weight is unequally supported by those that remain sound. The cause of this decay is owing to the neglect of the gutters and the lead-work over the lantern chamber and other parts of the lantern, which has either been improperly repaired or quite neglected for several years past, and ... I find that many hundreds of lead have been added to patch and hide what otherwise might have been repaired at less expense, so that much of the work is now covered with lead that was never intended to be so ... The windows in general are so bad and loaded with lead that it is impossible to repair them. The roof over the lantern chamber is so bad that hardly any water can get off it, and the kerb on which it rests is so decayed that the whole roof should be taken up and laid with a proper declivity to carry off the water. There are likewise two turrets that want re-building, one of them particularly is unsafe, having very little hold (and) may be blown down.

Essex fortunately decided to concentrate on the Octagon and Lantern first, but began his work in a very surprising way. His first action was to remove the large posts of timber let into slots at the eight internal corners of the stone tower, prepared by Alan of Walsingham's masons. These beams were the starting points for the wooden structure which had supported the floor of the roof-space, the roof itself, and the decorative vaulting which hid the sixteen raking shores, which in their turn supported the Lantern itself. To replace the removed timber, Essex placed stone corbels in

One end of one of Essex's supports for the floor of the roof-space, making use of the 'O' window and a suitable packing piece

the wall-slots at the appropriate heights to support (a) the new roof to the Octagon at its new, steeper inclination, and (b) the floor of the roof space and the decorative vaulting attached to it. As a means of supporting the floor while the corbels were being constructed, Essex seems to have used ingenious 'squinches' across each of the internal corners of the stone tower, comprised of beams which are placed between the lower sills of the two 'O' windows which adjoin each corner. (By 'squinches', I mean the kind of supports that are built into the corners of bell towers to support the base of, say, a spire.)

I am assuming that by using jacks and wedges, the floor could have been raised or lowered at each corner in turn, to facilitate the placing of the stone corbels in the wall slots after the wall timbers had been removed. There are accordingly eight large beams and sixteen adjustment wedges, which still supplement Essex's new supports in a real 'belt and braces' situation. On close examination it seems that each of the original eight 'fans' of flooring joists

Sketched diagram, looking east. Showing on the right, Alan of Walsingham's arrangement of supports for the Lantern, and on the left, Essex's revisions (black). The great oaks are red, the shores, green, the vaulting is gold, and the floor of the roof space is in blue. Note Essex's steeper roof line, removal of the exterior buttress (yellow) [replaced by Scott in the 1870s] and provision of corbels to replace the timber supports previously between the floor and roof of the Octagon roofspace (brown). Note too how the floor joists have been shortened and are supported by a substantial extra beam between the new corbel and the raking shore. To facilitate repairs to the feet of the raking shores, Essex provided duplicate 'shores' in addition to replacing the rotten ends to the originals.

which once were supported by the timber posts in the masonry slots, now stop short of each corner. These stubs of the old floor joists are now supported by Essex's 'squinches', while new beams of larger proportions now support the strengthened floor assembly using Essex's new corbels in the stonework at their outer end and new joints to the raking shores at their inner end.

According to George Gilbert Scott, who restored the Octagon approximately one hundred years after Essex, Essex seemed to have retained as much of the original structure as possible and

A slightly hazy enlargement from a view taken before the nineteenth-century restoration. Essex's 'gothic pavilion' from the southwest. Note the absence of stone pinnacles on the eight stairwells of the Octagon tower after Essex's restoration. Picture courtesy of The Wisbech and Downland Museum.

indeed all authorities seem agreed that all the sixteen raking shores are the original timbers installed under Hurley's supervising eye, just as the eight enormous oaks still form the frame of the Lantern. How then did Essex overcome the problem of the seven or eight shores that had rotted at the base? It seems that he inserted new bases, added to the lower ends of the shores to make good the required dimensions, and for good measure in what looks like another belt and braces solution, he duplicated those shores with extra shores above the originals. In addition, it seems to me that he has in effect transferred some of the weight of the roof to a strengthened floor, via some vertical supports, perhaps to relieve strain on the original shores which undoubtedly, as built, carried at least half of the original roof weight, as well as the Lantern itself. Essex's strengthened floor beams are also jointed firmly into the raking shores.

The structure still holds mysteries for us, but this is part of its fascination. It is very clear that Essex saved the Octagon from collapse by his inspired efforts, just as he went on to rescue the east end wall and its roof, and we owe him a considerable debt of gratitude.

Although retaining much of the original timber in the structure itself Essex changed the outward appearance of the Lantern quite considerably. The substantial casings that had protected the eight great oaks since the original construction were removed, as were the flying buttresses which braced them to the stone fabric of the Octagon itself. The windows and frames that Essex found to be in such disastrous condition were entirely removed and clear glass panes were fitted using a very simple tracery style. The angle of the roof between the tower and the Lantern was increased and the main windows were consequently shortened by about three feet. The windows to the bell chamber were also modified and similarly fitted with clear glass, while the substantial turrets protecting the tops of the eight great oaks were replaced with quite slender wooden pinnacles. The overall effect was, to my mind, much lighter in spirit, and from early photographs one can see the light streaming through the Lantern from all sides. Although Essex's plans seem to have envisaged that stone pinnacles would be added to the tops of the eight stone stairwells, in fulfilment of Alan of Walsingham's original intention, once again, fate or finance decreed otherwise and as we know those pinnacles were only eventually provided by Scott some one hundred years later.

If we wish to judge how Essex's Lantern looked from the interior of the Octagon, then in my view the watercolour by J. M. W. Turner of 1796 or so, gives us the best impression (see page 74). Essex had removed the *pulpitum* and the walls of the choir enclosure in 1769 and relocated the choir at the far east end of the presbytery, and the Octagon floor was now a clear and uncluttered space. Turner's picture shows a 'nave sermon' being delivered to the congregation while they sit on their own chairs and benches that by old custom were stored in the south transept when not in use. I particularly like the two tiny figures depicted standing high above the congregation on the precarious looking gallery just below the base of the Lantern windows. Similarly the Dean is shown as a minute figure preaching his sermon from the pulpit which in those days was just west of the then choir screen and two bays east of the eastern arch of the Octagon. The relics of the Saxon benefactors, displaced from the choir wall, were cremated and buried in Bishop West's chapel at the extreme southeast corner of the cathedral.

Essex's restoration had been of the nature of a last ditch rescue, but the Victorian restoration of the Octagon and Lantern which was to follow about a century later had only a lesser engineering component, and from the outset was intended to 'return the Octagon and Lantern to something approaching their mediaeval form'. The nineteenth-century restoration of Ely Cathedral had been originally inspired by George Peacock, a brilliant mathematics professor from Cambridge who had been appointed Dean in 1839. To get the measure of this man, one only needs to read a letter he sent to a close friend in 1816 when he wrote – 'I assure you that I shall never cease to exert myself to the utmost in the cause of reform and that I will never decline any office which may increase my power to effect it'.

Some twenty-three years later, his enthusiasm for reform and change undimmed, he set about improving the cathedral and environs. He wrote to George Gilbert Scott in 1847, to offer him the work associated with the removal of the choir to its present position, and Scott stayed on throughout the next twenty years or so of the great restoration. Peacock died in November 1858, before it could all be completed, and it was decided that the restoration of the Octagon and Lantern would be completed as his memorial. Scott accordingly launched an appeal to raise the funds, with the avowed intent as previously stated to 'return the Octagon and Lantern to something approaching their mediaeval form'. Freemans of Ely, a local builder, won the contract for the structural work, and it was carried out in 1862 and 1863. Scott prepared very careful drawings of the structure of the Octagon and Lantern and came to the conclusion that Essex in all his alterations had retained a great deal of the original structure and timber, despite his radical repairs. Scott satisfied himself that he could replicate the original tracery of the mediaeval windows from traces which he said were still in the framework, and went on to make a strong case for the restoration of the wooden flying buttresses which could be seen in early engravings depicting the original form of the Lantern. In addition he returned the roofline to the original lower mediaeval profile and in doing so of course enlarged the windows by some three feet, which restored them to the original dimensions intended by Alan of Walsingham. Scott and the head carpenter made the perilous journey up the ladder to the top of the Lantern itself, to satisfy himself that bells had originally been placed in the large chamber above the upper Lantern vault, and once satisfied, he designed bell slats for the window spaces that Essex had glazed

The Lantern as reinstated by Scott. The tops of two of the oak flying buttresses can just be seen at the bottom of the picture. The great oaks are hidden from view within lead-covered casings.

with plain glass. He was also intent to prove that the bell chamber on the Lantern was part of the original structure and this he said was easily shown because identical carpenters marks continued on up into the top chamber. The bells had been rung from a position in the south transept and grooves worn in the topmost beams of the bell chamber suggested that at least four bell ropes had been thus directed to the ringing position in the south transept.

The upper forty-three-foot-long sections of the eight great oaks were once again protected by lead-covered casings in imitation of the pre-Essex depictions of the tower, and finally despite quite a lot of heated discussion Scott put back massive flying buttresses of oak covered with lead. He triumphantly pointed out that the original mortises in the great angle posts themselves showed the position of the original mediaeval wooden buttresses.

The stonework of the Octagon tower was embellished with pinnacles and extra tracery on the balustrade, while the tops of the eight stairwells finally received their always intended, but never

The larger pinnacle (centre left) is atop one of the eight stairwells, while the more slender pinnacle (centre right) is centred along one of the long sides of the Octagon, in association with the re-instated oak buttress (far left). Note the extra tracery of the balustrade.

previously afforded pinnacles, complete with grotesques, hooded monks and dragons. For good measure Scott added four thinner, squarer, pinnacles at the centre of the four longer sides of the tower, presumably to take some of the thrust from the newly re-inserted buttresses on the four longer sides of the Octagon. As part of this operation Scott added eight vertical wooden beams bolted to the interior walls of the tower at the centre points of each of the eight sides to provide a seat for the new buttresses. Scott's drawings for this work helpfully label the surrounding timbers as 'old' where provided by Alan or Essex.

In the interior of the Lantern, Scott took down the tiny and precarious gallery that ran round the base of the windows, presumably when the windows were lengthened in the operation to change the angle of the roof. This little gallery is shown in several depictions of the interior of the Octagon, notably that watercolour by J. M. W. Turner of the nave sermon in progress in the 1790s, but I have not been able to establish if it was a mediaeval creation or part of Essex's improvements in the eighteenth-century restoration. On balance it seems to me that if Scott thought it was part of the original construction, he would have felt bound to keep it, and restore it. It may be too that Essex created it as part of the work to shorten the windows—it is certainly hard to see it coexisting with the previous longer windows of the original build.

To bring our account of the Octagon into the twentieth century, we need next to record the dramas of the early 1950s, when death-watch beetle threatened the roofs of the cathedral, together with the oak skeleton of the lantern and the lower vaulting of the Octagon roof. It was said that some of the curved oak ribs of the lower vaulting had been so badly attacked by the insects that they were almost eaten back to the level of the wooden boarding itself. Scaffolding was hurriedly erected to prevent a possible collapse of the structure, and even some of the eight great corner posts were said to be in great need of remedial work. Fortunately, some spectacular posters showing Ely being attacked by giant beetles caught the public imagination and their generosity showed how much affection and esteem was available to be turned into hard cash to remedy the position.

The twenty-fifth of January 1990 saw another dramatic event in the history of the Octagon, when a huge storm sweeping across the fens began to loosen some of the windows of the Lantern and seriously damaged the lead roof. Once again, saintly protectors seem to have sprung into action, because very fortuitously, workmen and ladders were on site, and two very brave men were able to secure the windows before major damage occurred.

A plaque on the roof records that the lead was repaired and restored in 1991.

The end of the twentieth century saw the Victorian decorations of the Octagon and Lantern cleaned and restored as part of the major restoration of the cathedral as a whole between 1986 and 2000. I feel it is necessary to record the devotion and perseverance of the restorers who apparently cleaned Thomas Gambier Parry's paintwork with cotton buds and detergent, an inch at a time!

The Decoration and Imagery of the Octagon and Lantern

When we look at the interior sculptures and painted decoration of the 'new work', completed by Alan of Walsingham in 1342, we must bear in mind that the ravages of the Reformation and the attendant 'image breaking' have altered the look of the Octagon considerably since then. The painted decoration and the angels are nineteenth-century, and even some of the statuary has been replaced in Victorian times, albeit with fairly good evidence that the replacement is entirely appropriate.

The huge floor space at the crossing, which present day Ely finds so useful for important services and concerts, was simply not intended to be so by Alan, who was only intent on restoring the monks' choir inside its enclosure at the centre of the church. The new monks' choir extended from just east of the old *pulpitum* (a screen built across the nave, at that time one bay from the opening into the Octagon), to St Peter's altar which intruded by one bay into the new work of Bishop Hotham's bays. The north and south walls of the choir were replaced on their original alignment, and Alan replaced the relics of the seven Saxon benefactors in their old position in the north wall, so that their tombs would be immediately in front of the pilgrims who, as we know, customarily entered the cathedral through the northwest door in the north transept.

Above these tombs were representations of the occupants, painted on the wall, and miraculously, through the indefatigable efforts of eighteenth- and nineteenth-century antiquarians, we have details of them. James Essex demolished the *pulpitum* and the walls of the old monks' choir in May 1769, in order to move the choir to the far east end of the presbytery. The spacious dimensions of the Octagon were revealed for the first time since Alan had supervised the re-erection of the monks' choir in the 1340s.

When the Octagon was first completed, considerable statuary

*The carved head of a queen
(one of the mortals)*

Just a king, or Edward II?

*A grotesque (one of the
sixteen carved heads)*

and sculpture adorned the walls, and as we examine the evidence it seems apparent that the tower and its domed roof was intended to be a glorious shrine to St Etheldreda, our founding saint, and to the various Saxon benefactors who had given gifts of land to ensure the foundation's success. Excluding purely painted decoration, dating from the nineteenth century, there are no less than nine 'levels' of symbolic statuary and carvings in the Octagon, rising from the ends of the hood moulds on the smaller aisle arches, to the wooden carving of Jesus at the very centre of the highest visible vaulting in the centre. In order from the floor of the crossing they are:

- Heads of 'mortals' (king, queen, bishop, prior, monk and artisan, also 'good' and 'evil' represented by respectively a lion and a grotesque imp). All these heads are at the 'hood mould' ends (the raised ribs just above the aisle arches).
- The Etheldreda sculptures at the foot of the empty niches showing scenes from her life and the miracles that occurred.
- The empty niches themselves and their occupants lost at the Reformation.
- Twelve seated apostles in the tented canopies (Victorian replacements).
- The heads of sixteen Old Testament prophets placed between the apostles.
- Just above the apostles and the prophets and below the 'battlemented' sills of the four windows of the tower proper, there is a line of small carved heads of unknown attribution. There are sixteen in all. There are, among others, grotesques and devils, men and women, and no particular theme seems to emerge.
- The four evangelists in niches at the top of the four large crossing arches.
- The eight crowned heads, carved in wood around the base of the Lantern.
- Jesus, at the highest visible point of the Lantern. He is displaying his crucifixion wounds in his hands and in his right side.

At the ends of the hood-moulds (raised ribs immediately above an arch) of the smaller aisle arches into the Octagon, we find 'mortals', and 'good and evil' represented. Starting at the northwest aisle arch we see, to the left, a monk or clerical person, and on the right, a layman or artisan with long hair and a beard and moustache. In the northeast aisle, a queen and a king, and in the

The northeast aisle arch of the Octagon showing the disposition of the lowest six levels of sculpture: (A) carved heads; (B) prophets; (C) apostles; (D) empty niches (martyr saints?); (E) Etheldreda sculptures (left: 'Etheldreda Taking the Veil at Coldingham', right: 'The Miracle of the Sprouting Staff'); (F) mortals (left: queen, right: king).

southeast, a bishop and a prior. The southwest aisle arch displays a lion's head and a hooded figure, customarily held here to represent 'good and evil' respectively. In the nineteenth century and earlier, it was routine to attribute these likenesses to actual folk associated with the building of the Octagon; the monk became Alan of Walsingham, while the layman or artisan became William Hurley the master carpenter, or more likely in view of the date, perhaps the master mason John of Ramsey. Similarly the bishop and prior became Hotham and Crauden respectively. The king and queen were also said to be Edward III and Queen Phillipa, and in this way the whole attribution was endangered because Edward III had not succeeded to the throne until 1327, and we know the stone part of the tower was all but complete by 1328. It seems more appropriate to regard these small heads as merely representative human categories (though I could add, mischievously, that the king bears a quite remarkable resemblance to the effigy of Edward II on his tomb at Gloucester).

As we raise our gaze to the foot of the eight, large, empty niches, we see tiny scenes crowded with figures, and these represent the life and miracles of St Etheldreda. They are symbolically placed a little higher than the ordinary mortals of the hood moulds. Given their subject matter, these are to my mind a truly miraculous survival, because often the image breakers of the Reformation were particularly conscientious in removing all traces of local saints. Bishop Goodrich, the incumbent at the time of the Reformation, seems to have developed a 'blind spot' around these carvings, and it has been speculated too that Etheldreda's royal birth may have influenced proceedings. In any event they have survived and they continue to display Etheldreda's superiority over mere mortals. Goodrich is reputed to have convinced Mary I that throughout the Reformation he had remained a 'good Catholic', to the effect that she allowed him to remain Bishop of Ely, so perhaps mental gymnastics came easily to him.

The sculptures themselves have given rise to a lot of discussion about the scenes they purport to show, and two in particular seem to stir up controversy, whilst the sequence in which they are displayed seems at first sight to be incorrect.

My own attributions of subjects to the sculptures are as follows, starting at the western side of the arch into the north transept and proceeding clockwise:

1 The marriage of Etheldreda to Tondberht (her first husband who died after only two years and bequeathed to her the Isle of Ely).
2 Etheldreda taking the veil at Coldingham after being released from her second marriage by her husband Ecgfrith, King of Northumbria.
3 The miracle of the sprouting staff. Resting on a grassy bank after eluding her husband at St Abb's Head, her staff took root overnight and burst into bloom.
4 The miracle at St Abb's Head. Ecgfrith was prevented by an unusually high and persistent tide from capturing Etheldreda, who had taken refuge on the promontory.
5 Etheldreda appointed Abbess at Ely in AD 673.
6 Etheldreda's death and first burial in AD 679.
7 The miracle of Byrhtstan's release. (This is a much later miracle from the reign of Henry I and the last in the chronological sequence. Byrhtstan, a usurer, was thrown into jail on false evidence. He prayed to St Etheldreda and St Benedict, and vowed to become a monk at Ely if he was released. The sculpture shows

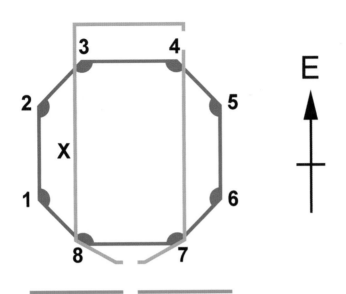

The positions of the Etheldreda sculptures in the Octagon (in red), with the choir enclosure (in blue) shown as rebuilt by Alan of Walsingham. The pulpitum (or screen) is also shown (in green). The relics of seven Saxon benefactors were re-buried in the outer face of the north wall of the choir at X.

his miraculous release from his symbolic cell. For many years his discarded fetters or boies were displayed very even-handedly halfway between the shrine of St Etheldreda and the altar of St Benedict.)

8 The miraculous discovery of Etheldreda's uncorrupted body after sixteen years in the ground. This, her first 'translation', was in AD 695.

Whichever way these tableaux are read, clockwise or in reverse, they do not form a chronological sequence unless one separates them into (a) the miracles 3, 4, 7, and 8, and secondly (b) the scenes from Etheldreda's life and death in 1, 2, 5, and 6.

It occurs to me that if one reimposes the original outline of the stalls of the monks' choir on the Octagon,[18] the sculptures most easily seen from within that enclosure are the four 'miracles', 3, 4, 7, and 8. Similarly from outside the choir, the pilgrims and lay folk would more easily see the 'life scenes' 1, 2, 5, and 6.

Intriguingly, the life scenes can be read in perfectly correct chronological sequence, in a clockwise direction starting at the pillar on the northwest side of the north transept, whilst the miracles can be read in sequence if read anticlockwise starting at the pillar on the south side of the opening into the eastern arm of the church, i.e. in the sequence 4, 3, 8, and 7.

What I want to suggest here is that the dispositions of the various scenes around the Octagon columns might have something to do with the way the pilgrims circulated around the church.

18 See *A History of Ely Cathedral*, ed. P. Meadows and N. Ramsay (Woodbridge, The Boydell Press, 2003), Plate 8(c). Photomontage by Edward Maddison of the fourteenth-century stalls relocated in the Octagon space.

Long tradition tells us that they entered by the door at the north-west corner of the north transept and went first to the tombs of the Saxon benefactors, hard by the first of the pillar sculptures in the life sequence—'the marriage of Etheldreda to Tondberht' (1). They would pass 'Etheldreda taking the veil' (2) and proceed to the new Lady chapel and from thence to the shrines, maybe leaving eventually past 'Etheldreda appointed as Abbess at Ely' (5) and 'Death and burial of Etheldreda' (6). Passing around the west end of the monk's choir, but to the east of the *pulpitum*, they could perhaps have exited again via the northwest door.

Michael E. Goodich, in *Violence and Miracle in the Fourteenth Century* (1995) pages 18 and 19, comments on cultic processions in the 1340s as follows:

> Considerable variation characterised such processions. While the parish or quarter as a whole may be considered a sacred space by virtue of the saint after which it was named, a specially defined geography of the sacred found expression in the circuit followed by the religious procession. Certain persons, dates, places, and objects are 're-sanctified' in the course of the festivities, while others, given their secondary involvement, suffer exclusion or institutionalised disenfranchisement. The route of the procession may be of two kinds: either enclosed, that is, beginning and ending in the same place, generally the site of the relics, and encompassing major civic spaces, such as the church, cemetery, public square or monastery, or linear one street or byway, joining the end points of the town or village.

As to why the correct chronological sequence of the miracles within the choir relies on an anticlockwise reading, I can only suggest that the arrangement of the miracles in that order does leave the most important miracles at the end of the choir where the bishop and the prior sat.

I have to acknowledge that the whole elaborate construct falls to the ground if my attribution of subjects to sculptures is not entirely correct and over the years distinguished observers have voiced other opinions. For example James Bentham, our historian of the eighteenth century, suggested that the first sculpture 'Marriage to Tondberht' was actually Etheldreda's second marriage to Prince Ecgfrith,[19] and pointed out that Bishop Wilfrid is shown as officiating, and he would not have been present at Tondberht's nuptials. The sculpture we see however shows very clearly that the groom has a full beard and since Ecgfrith was only fifteen or so it seems likely that Tondberht is the intended husband in this sculpture (he was reputed to be fifty-eight at that time). It would also be important, as Phillip Lindley[20] points out, that

19 See James Bentham, *The History and Antiquities of the Conventual & Cathedral Church of Ely* (Cambridge, Cambridge University Press, 1812), p. 48 & Plate IX.
20 See Phillip Lindley, 'The Imagery of the Octagon at Ely', *Journal of the British Archaeological Association*, 139 (1986), p. 80.

'Etheldreda's First Marriage to Tondberht'? The first corbel in the 'life' sequence. Northwest aisle arch, northern side (position 1).

Tondberht's settlement of the Isle of Ely on Etheldreda 'in dower', should be referred to in any life of the saint, and it may be that the groom in this tableaux is carrying a scroll or documents in a bag to indicate the pre-nuptial agreement.

The King and Queen are shown forcing a reluctant Etheldreda to 'take the hand' of Tondberht.

Whichever groom is shown here, however, the basic sequence of events is not upset and both of the competing interpretations of the scene depicted on this corbel are consistent with our overall account of the series. But it is not so easy to reconcile my 'miracles' theory with both of the conflicting interpretations of the problematic sculpture we turn to next.

I refer to the eighth corbel in my list above, which if accepted as the 'miraculous discovery of Etheldreda's uncorrupted body', after sixteen years in the ground, it becomes the third miracle in the series of four. The corbel is situated on the southern side of the northwest aisle arch.

Recently, the long accepted attribution that this was Etheldreda's first translation has been questioned on the grounds that it would not have been acceptable to portray her as naked to the waist in such an indiscreet way. The proponents of this view suggest that this carving shows the death of Tondberht, and that Etheldreda is shown at the bedside.

I have studied the photograph in conjunction with the description of the miraculous discovery as described in Janet Fairweather's excellent translation of the *Liber Eliensis* (the Book of

'Translation of Etheldreda in 695', or 'Death of Tondberht'? Northwest aisle arch, western side (position 8).

Ely, page 59 et seq., see Select Bibliography), which makes the event come alive. I think I see more points of correspondence with the translation theory, although it has to be said that the body does appear to have some suggestion of a prominent jaw-line, which some might see as a beard—but I think this refers to the cloth over the face. Indeed this covering of the face is mentioned quite specifically at line 13 on page 60 of Janet Fairweather's translation of *Liber Eliensis*. Cynefrith (Etheldreda's physician just before she died) says:

> And when the covering of her face was removed, they showed me also that the wound of the incision which I had made, had been healed, in such a way that instead of the open gaping wound with which she was buried, there appeared at that time the slightest traces of a scar.

However, to compare the entire scene on the corbel with Janet Fairweather's translation, we need to go back to line 23 of page 59:

> So a tent awning having been fixed up and arranged in a seemly manner over the place, as the whole congregation, brothers on one side, sisters on the other, were standing around the grave singing psalms. — And the holy Abbess Seaxburh, after the casket-lid had been opened, went in with a few people, as if to raise the bones and shake them apart, and after there had been a short pause, we suddenly heard her call out from inside in a loud voice — 'Glory be to the most high name of the Lord!'

Cynefrith says:

> And so that these things might be made public in the confirmatory presence
> of witnesses, a little while later they called me inside too, and I saw, raised
> from the tomb and placed on a couch, the body of the holy virgin, looking
> like someone asleep.

My own view is that the corbel sculpture portrays the exact
moment that Seaxburh calls out, for we see Cynefrith just outside
the door of the tent with his hand raised to his right ear as if
hearing the shout. To his right we see a collection of notables and
'the great and the good' who were specifically invited to witness
the event, and most convincingly of all we can pick out Wilfrid,
who would not have been present at the death of Tondberht. In my
view the Abbess figure is Seaxburh, and I see her pose as
indicating Etheldreda's neck which has miraculously healed. If this
is so, then the figure here is correctly shown as an Abbess and a
Queen, because Seaxburh had been Queen of Kent until her
husband's death. If the sculptor intended to portray Etheldreda
here, at the time of Tondberht's death, neither the crown nor the
Abbess' headress would have been appropriate.

As to Etheldreda's grave clothes, it is very difficult to see
whether she is portrayed as naked to the waist. I think I can make
out a seam of material, which is draped over Etheldreda's right
shoulder and continues under her left arm, presumably to place on
show the healed wound. It occurs to me that the 'modesty' issue is
dealt with anyway by the 'tent arranged in a seemly manner', and
after all, at that stage, Etheldreda was only being inspected by her
sister and her doctor. It did occur to me to volunteer to clean the
sculpture from the moveable scaffold, so that I could get a really
close look at the central figure on its couch. My photograph does
reveal some substantial cobwebs. It seems inconceivable that any
sculptural account of Etheldreda's well-merited sainthood would
omit an impressive mention of her body being found uncorrupted
after sixteen years in the grave, and none of the other corbels could
really be interpreted as referring to her translation.

The only other carving which has been offered as an alternative
for the translation scene in 695, is number six on my list, i.e. 'The
Death and First Burial of Etheldreda', which is situated on the
south side of the southwest aisle arch. My first objection to that
'burial' attribution being changed to 'translation' would be that the
two halves of the corbel are clearly intended to show two closely
linked events. The left side of the carving shows Etheldreda on her

'Death of Etheldreda and First Burial'. Southwest aisle arch, southern side (position 6).

deathbed, and the scene on the right shows her in what looks to me to be a good representation of a wooden coffin with a flat lid in which she was buried in her ordinary grave in the cemetery in 679. The 'white marble' coffin from Grantcaestir (Cambridge), used for her first translation in 695, which Henry VIII's commissioners gleefully found to be ordinary stone, would no doubt have been more of the Roman kind with thickish walls and a cavity shaped for the head. So, on balance, I am not at all convinced that this is her first translation. *Liber Eliensis*, the Book of Ely, says of the miraculously discovered stone coffin, 'the place set apart for the head also appeared most suitably configured'. Elsewhere the book refers to the miracle of her body found uncorrupted, as 'A stupendous, extraordinary miracle, and one to be proclaimed for all eternity'.

Altogether perhaps, a miracle that requires more 'column inches' than half a corbel, and which merits its display at the west end of the choir on the northwest aisle arch as number three in a series of four miracles which underwrite Etheldreda's valid and powerful claim to sainthood. In the first quarter of the fourteenth century it would have been most important to restate clearly proof of St Etheldreda's saintliness. The Church was beginning to evolve

'Etheldreda Installed as Abbess of Ely'. Southeast aisle arch, southern side (position 5).

'The Miracle of Byrhtstan's Release from Prison by St Benedict and St Etheldreda'. Southwest aisle arch, western side (position 7).

new standards of evidence against which all miracle events were to be tested, and our four miracle sculptures should, I think, be examined in that light.[21]

To enable all the Etheldreda sculptures to be compared at the same time, in the same publication, I list and display the other five reliefs in the following pages.

The next level of sculpture asks more questions than can be answered with any certainty. I refer to the eight large empty niches just above the eight Etheldreda corbels. The niches themselves are of interest in that they display so much common design ground with similar features in the Lady chapel, and Prior Crauden's chapel. To me, these niches represent another reminder that Alan

21 See Michael E. Goodich, *Violence and Miracle in the Fourteenth Century: Private Grief and Public Salvation* (Chicago, The University of Chicago Press, 1995), pp 6–18.

'Etheldreda Taking the Veil at Coldingham'. Northeast aisle arch, northern side (position 2).

'The Miracle of the Sprouting Staff'. Northeast aisle arch, eastern side (position 3).

'The Miracle of St Abbs Head'. Southeast aisle arch, eastern side (position 4).

of Walsingham made enormous attempts to harmonise his 'new work' with the work of the previous builders of the church by picking up on the design themes they had employed. The columns bisecting the backs of the niches are a charming echo of those that appear in Romanesque arches on the west front of the southwest transept and in niches in the Lady chapel.

T. D. Atkinson,[22] the cathedral architect in the thirties, says the Octagon niches are made of Thevesdale stone from Yorkshire, the same quarry that provided much of the stone for York Minster.

The niches are very shallow and this has led to arguments that they were too narrow to accommodate statuary. Viewed from above, from say the north transept at tribune level, the base of the niche shows ample room for a figure, and indeed the niche in the southeast corner has slight damage to its bisecting column which may suggest a fixing point to secure just such a figure. Phillip Lindley, in his paper 'The Imagery of the Octagon at Ely', says that fragments of statues of the appropriate dimensions exist in the stone store in Ely's north nave tribune. The largest fragment is the torso of a man apparently holding a scroll. We cannot therefore know the theme of these niches' occupants. They may relate to the general theme of 'benefactors' to the cathedral, or as Phillip Lindley suggests, the eight niches may have contained figures of 'martyr saints'.[23]

Just above the tops of the eight empty niches, in the centres of the walls above the four aisle arches, we find the twelve apostles in four sections of three, enclosed in canopied niches. St Paul has been substituted for Judas Iscariot, it seems. At the four lower extremities of each canopy, we can see four mediaeval carved heads, which seem to represent prophets of the Old Testament, and there are thus sixteen prophets shown. Old pictures of the Octagon, again notably J. M. W. Turner's watercolour of 1796, show that these 'tented canopies' were empty, having been attacked by the image breakers. An eminent Victorian sculptor, J. E. Redfern, was able to convince himself that the niches had contained seated figures of the apostles and provided suitable replacements in the period from 1868 to 1876. Suggestions have been made recently that the details of the apostles' figures are so fine that they may be moulded in plaster. The contemporary guidebook (1874 edition) says they were 'executed in stone'.

For the last level of stone statuary in the Octagon, we have to try to reach a vantage point where we can peer into the dusty recesses at the very top of the four high arches where the Octagon

An empty niche. One of eight situated on the walls above the four aisle arches.

22 See T. D. Atkinson, *An Architectural History of the Benedictine Monastery of St Etheldreda at Ely*, p. 39 and footnote.

23 See Phillip Lindley, 'The Imagery of the Octagon at Ely', pp 75–99.

adjoins the nave, both transepts, and the present choir. In four small niches just above the arches themselves we find the four evangelists, seated at small desks and writing with quill pens we are told. In this instance we will have to rely on hearsay, because it is almost impossible to see any detail in the gloom under the corners of the lower vaulting, except to make out their names inscribed beneath. Their lonely perches at such giddy height did not however save them from the image breakers of the Reformation. Some brave and zealous soul found a way to scale the heights and smash their heads. St Matthew is atop the arch to the north transept, St Mark in the arch to the east, St Luke to the south, and St John to the west. The evangelists were renovated and repaired during the Victorian redecoration of the Octagon and Lantern.

The next level of carving in the Octagon is displayed at the lower edge of the sill on which the Lantern stands. I have not seen any references to these wooden carvings, but they seem to represent crowned heads. They are at such a distance from the observer on the ground, that they tend to be missed against the overall beauty of the vaulted ceiling, whilst from the 'angel doors' in the Lantern itself, only the tops of the crowns are visible. Closer inspection reveals strange and archaic figures with masses of curly hair and wild eyes. They are clearly intended to represent eight very different monarchs, and given the featuring of King Edgar the first king of all England in the original stained glass of the Octagon windows, I can only suggest that these are the eight kings who it is said showed their fealty to Edgar by rowing him down the

Above: St Jude, St James (major) and St Simon on the wall above the northeast aisle arch with Old Testament companions between them wearing symbolic prophets' headgear. The attributions of the other aisle arches are: northwest arch, St Thomas, St Peter and St Andrew; southeast arch, St Matthew, St John and St James (minor); southwest arch, St Philip, St Paul and St Bartholomew.

Opposite: Interior of Ely Cathedral - looking Towards the North Transept and Chancel by J. M. W. Turner (1796). Aberdeen Art Gallery & Museums Collections.

One of the wild-eyed kings at the base of the Lantern

River Dee at Chester in AD 973. Sir Frank Stenton in his *Anglo-Saxon England* (1971) says that the annalist Florence of Worcester names them as Kenneth, King of Scots, Malcolm, King of the Cumbrians, Maccus, King of Many Islands, Dufnal, Siferth, Huwal, Jacob, and Juchil. The assembled kings apparently rowed Edgar from his palace to the church of St John and back again, while he in lordly fashion took the tiller. (After I had made several unsuccessful attempts at photographing these sculptures, a guiding colleague pointed out that there is already a fine photograph of the kings in the Chapter office, just above the photocopier.)

This event would have been regarded as vitally important at Ely because the peace of Edgar's unchallenged reign was the breathing space required to set in train his revival of religious establishments, of which of course Ely was one. Edgar had set about bringing monasticism in this country up to Continental standards and had gone so far as to import books and writings from Europe to re-order the rules by which monasteries were administered. Chief among the monasteries consulted was Fleury, which had already been reformed to the latest specifications and had the authority bestowed on it by being home to St Benedict's bones. Many English houses borrowed literature from Fleury and copied items extensively for their own use, while Ethelwold, Ely's re-founder, went so far as to translate the Rule of St Benedict from Fleury into Anglo-Saxon because it was clear to him that the knowledge of ecclesiastical Latin was rare in Britain. Confirmation of this is available from *Liber Eliensis*[24] where it is recorded that Ethelwold was rewarded for this task by the grant of the manor of Southburne in Suffolk, by Edgar himself.

References to Edgar by way of the windows and the sculptures honour the fact that even the rules governing behaviour in the community were shaped by him and his advisors.

The final carving to examine is in the upper vaulting of the Lantern, and I refer of course to the central wooden boss itself, the carving of Christ displaying his crucifixion wounds. Carved by John of Burwell for the princely sum of 'two shillings (or ten pence), and his keep at the Abbot's table', it was likely erected in late 1339 or so, when two shillings seems to have equated to about £100 at today's rates (in strict retail price appreciation terms). Even this seems slight reward for such a work, and comparative values seem notoriously hard to calculate over such long periods. As an alternative comparison, I recall that an archer at the battle of Crecy in 1346 earned about *2d.* a day, while the Black Prince, Edward III's

24 See Janet Fairweather, *Liber Eliensis, A History of the Isle of Ely from the Seventh Century to the Twelfth Compiled by a Monk of Ely in the Twelfth Century* (Woodbridge, Boydell, 2005), book ii, para. 37.

The central boss of the Lantern some one hundred and forty-two feet above the crossing. It measures approximately 4 feet 4 inches across, from the tip of the halo to the base of the clouds.

son, earned about 19*s*. a day fighting for his father.

The central boss was recut and restored in 1874, as part of the nineteenth-century restoration. One tale has it that, in less reverential times, part of the church had been used to breed pigeons, and when a bird escaped and became a nuisance in the Lantern, they would shoot it down, to the detriment of the fabric.

Once again there are conflicting versions of the dimensions of that central boss. At various times it has been described as 'considerably bigger than life-size', or 'six feet across'. I did hear once (but haven't been able since to pin the story down) that it was lowered to the floor in the last major restoration of the Lantern and it was measured carefully, so maybe someone knows its correct dimensions. Having measured it, but only photographically, I make the diameter from the tip of the halo to the base of the clouds to be around 4 feet 4 inches (1.33 metres) on the basis that the internal diameter of the Lantern is 30 feet (9.23 metres).

Stained Glass in the Octagon and Lantern

All the stained glass that we see as we look round in the Octagon today is nineteenth-century glass, inserted between 1849 and 1871 by that famous maker William Wailes, under the auspices of Canon Edward Sparke who oversaw much of the stained glass renewals of those years. He was able to use the investments made with such foresight by his father, Bishop Bowyer Sparke, before his death in 1836. Apparently, £2,000 was invested in Government stocks and this sum appreciated so well, that it financed many of the nineteenth-century additions to the stained glass of the cathedral. The windows of the Lantern itself were installed as part of the memorial to Dean Peacock, and were added in 1863. They contain his initials, 'G.P.' and tiny peacocks as part of the design. The 1880 guidebook gives a summary of the amounts expended on the cathedral in the thirty years prior to its publication, and this includes some £10,022 spent on restoring the Lantern as a memorial to the late Dean Peacock, furnishing the Octagon, and filling the large windows with stained glass. Dean Peacock's many friends contributed some £2,407 to the memorial fund, and one wonders if this was a conscious effort to match the £2,406 6s. 11d. of the original cost of the building of the Octagon in 1342. As with almost all the 'improvements' of the nineteenth century, there were detractors. Some people disliked the 'rather garish' colours of the new Lantern windows, and it seems that Thomas Gambier Parry was prevailed upon to tone them down with a process he called 'enamelling' when he carried out the repainting of the Lantern in the 1870s.

We know very little about the original windows as provided by Alan of Walsingham in the original build of the stone tower and the Lantern. The sacrist roll for the year 1325–1326 mentions that in addition to all the normal building supplies for the new tower,

Opposite: One of the eight Lantern windows inserted in 1863 as a memorial to Dean George Peacock who died in 1858. Note his initials 'G.P.' and tiny peacocks.

Southeast window

UPPER TIER (left to right)
King Anna; Etheldreda as
Queen of Northumbria;
Tondberht; Ecgfrith.

LOWER TIER (left to right)
St Etheldreda as Abbess;
Wilfrid (Bishop of York);
St Ermenilda (third Abbess);
St Seaxburh (second Abbess).

'white glass, and colours for staining it were bought', so from that we can assume that some, if not all, of the tower windows were intended to be stained-glass windows. References to *canvasii* bought at Lenn (Lynn) suggest that temporary covers were used until the windows were ready to be inserted.

It also seems likely that those original stained-glass windows survived the 'image breaking' of the sixteenth century, because Essex reports that the windows could not be saved because they were in such a parlous condition. By a very fortunate circumstance, two sketches of the original designs survived in the collect-

Northeast window

*UPPER TIER (left to right)
Archbishop Dunstan;
St Werberga; St Edmund;
St Withburga.*

*LOWER TIER (left to right)
King Edgar; Abbot Brithnoth;
Brithnoth (earldoman of
Essex); Bishop Ethelwold (re-
founder of the Benedictine
monastery).*

ion of a famous antiquarian William Stukely (1687–1765), and they
show two kings—Edgar, under whose auspices the Monastery was
re-founded in AD 970 as a Benedictine establishment, and Ecgfrith,
King of Northumbria and Etheldreda's second husband.

Phillip Lindley points out that in the sacrist roll of 1349–1350
there is an entry for the repair of a window in the Octagon depicting King Edgar, so once again there is some happy confirmation. If
all the windows contained only images of royalty, then perhaps this
is why they may have been spared.

The subjects of the nineteenth century windows in the tower

Northwest window

UPPER TIER (left to right)
Edward II; Henry III; Henry I;
William I.

LOWER TIER (left to right)
Alan of Walsingham; Bishop
Northwold (builder of the
presbytery); Harvey (first
Bishop of Ely); Abbot Simeon
(first builder of the Norman
cathedral).

itself follow closely the theme of founders, benefactors, and royal associations which the Victorians adduced from the few clues left to them.

A detailed study of the northwest Octagon window, probably best carried out from the angel panels in the Lantern, shows three roundels of interest above the eight main figures. In the centre there is a representation of the shrine of St Etheldreda. To the left, Abbott Simeon is shown laying the foundation stone of the Cathedral. On the right we see Alan of Walsingham and the monks weeping over the ruins of the central tower. The arms of the

Southwest window

*UPPER TIER (left to right)
Queen Victoria; Prince Albert;
King Edward III; Queen
Phillipa.*

*LOWER TIER (left to right)
Bishop Turton; Dean
Peacock; Bishop Hotham;
Prior Crauden.*

University of Cambridge, the See of Ely and of Bishop Sparke witness that half the cost of this window was defrayed by graduates of the University and the other half by the money left by Bishop Sparke.

Queen Victoria and Prince Albert are depicted in the south-west window and the 1874 guidebook confirms that 'the cost of a portion of this window was graciously defrayed by Her Majesty while Bishop Turton and Dean Peacock gave the cost of their figures'.

The Victorian Repainting of the Octagon and Lantern

We have seen already that the original mediaeval painting scheme was lost under limewash for many years,[25] and faint traces of that scheme only came to light in 1850, when the limewash was removed as the great Victorian restoration began to gather pace. In the relatively short period of twenty-five years or so between then and 1875, when Thomas Gambier Parry executed his designs, there were various proposals made for a replacement scheme. A small section of the vaulting was restored as an experiment but this scheme was not completed, and Parry's first proposals came to nothing. Persistence brought its own reward however, for in the 1874 (September) guidebook, we find a passage which describes Parry's thought processes leading up to the final design which he executed in the following year.

The paragraph reads:

> On the entire restoration of the Octagon and Lantern in 1874, the artist's work has been entrusted to Mr Gambier-Parry. It is out of our power to describe what he is now doing, for the work was only begun as these pages were being printed. We understand from him that as the final illustration of sacred subjects on the nave was 'Christ in Glory', he could find no subject compatible with the architectural forms of the Lantern but that of a series of thirty-two single figures, filling the panels beneath the windows. These will form an illustration of the 150th Psalm: the figures will be angels playing instruments of music, such as were common at the period of the building, the middle of the fourteenth century, and the inscription beneath their feet will be the first verse of that Psalm, 'Praise God in His holiness, praise him in the firmament of his power'.

There is no trace of the inscription in the Lantern today, of course, but the above paragraph goes a long way to suggest that the idea to put angels in the Lantern was wholly Parry's and he was not simply replacing mediaeval designs.

Opposite: Three angels from the Lantern, painted by Thomas Gambier Parry

25 Celia Fiennes in *Illustrated Journeys of Celia Fiennes, 1685–1712*, ed. C. Morris (Exeter, Webbe Bower, 1982) says at p. 142, lines 18/19, 'The Lanthorn in ye quire is vastly high and delicately painted' (this is in 1698). The limewash seems to have been applied sometime between then and Turner's depiction of the Octagon in 1796 (see p. 74).

As one reads of this stage of the nineteenth century restoration, the conclusion dawns that Parry was a serious mediaevalist with fixed ideas about what was right and appropriate, even to his special formula for 'spirit fresco',[26] the paint that was intended to give the right colour palette for fourteenth-century subjects. He had previously found fault with the subject matter and style of the nave ceiling, which of course was the inspiration of his onetime schoolfriend Henry Styleman Lestrange, and further, went to great lengths to keep his final design for the Octagon and Lantern a secret, even from the supervising architect, Sir George Gilbert Scott.

Once again there were detractors. Amongst the critics was William Morris, who said in a letter to William Bryce in 1879 that he would likely have preferred Ely when it was all grey and venerable. He suggested that the Lantern had been 'daubed over like a music hall'. Presumably his comments followed a close inspection of the angels, because they are quite heavily outlined to give extra definition at the distances they are viewed from below. Close to, they appear rather like 'fairground' painting but have a distinctly ethereal, Pre-Raphaelite air when viewed from the floor of the crossing. An art restorer who visited us recently pointed out that the 'waist to feet' dimension of the angels has been increased to reduce the foreshortening effect of looking up at them at such a steep angle. It's obvious once you're told.

26 See page 106 for the formula for 'spirit fresco', otherwise known as 'the Ely medium'.

A Tour of the Octagon and Lantern

Not everyone relishes the effort involved in climbing to the roof of a cathedral by way of tiny spiral staircases and even tinier doors, so it seems to me that I should describe the main features of a tour of the Octagon and Lantern, in the hope that I may entice more adventurous visitors to come and see this truly amazing construction.

Most tours will begin at the west end of the cathedral in the nave, and from there one can get a sense of the great size of the cathedral, and some idea of the construction of that original stone tower which stood on its four huge pillars at the centre of the crossing. As we proceed down the nave we pass a plain grey slab of Purbeck marble[27] set in the floor in the centre aisle, which marks the burial site of Alan of Walsingham. The brasses are now missing, but in the faint engraved outline on the slab we can clearly see that Alan is depicted wearing a mitre. This is a reference to Alan's election by the whole community as Bishop of Ely in 1344. Sadly the Pope and the authorities appointed another candidate, Thomas de Lisle, but the monks seem to have been intent on making a point here. Another significant feature of the slab is the considerable space provided at Alan's feet for an epitaph of ten lines of poetry (for a translation, see the Author's Note). Strong evidence, it seems, that Alan was hugely respected and loved by the whole community when he died in 1363.

Sitting under the Octagon itself, we can revel in the beauty and glory of the star-shaped vaulting, which conceals the enormous oak beams that support the Lantern. We need to appreciate at this point that the huge wooden roof above us is about the same size as that gaping hole in the roof caused by the collapse of the original stone tower. The eight huge oak trees that form the vertical corners of the Lantern itself rest on the octagonal sill at the top of the lower vaulting. This sill is some hundred feet (thirty-three metres)

27 Not strictly a true marble in geological terms, but a hard, compressed, shelly limestone, which is capable of taking a good polish. It is found in Dorset as its name suggests, and it was *the* prestigious decorative stone of the thirteenth and fourteenth centuries.

The star-shaped vaulting of the Octagon and Lantern

above us. We know that Thomas Carpenter's famous crane lifted the components of the structure—but how?

Faced with a large discrepancy between the height of the vaulting in the ritual choir and the height of the arch into the Octagon, Alan designed a *supercilium*, or 'eyebrow', which he filled with elegant tracery. In the central space of this feature there is a faint depiction of the crucifixion.

Moving now towards the door to the Octagon tower in the northeast corner of the north transept, we can examine a simplified model of the Lantern construction inside the stone tower. To gain some sense of the essential simplicity of the original design, we must concentrate on the Lantern 'cylinder' comprising the eight huge oaks, standing on the original sixteen fourteenth-century supports, rooted into the eight stone columns of the tower. The model also contains references to some of the extra supports inserted during the eighteenth-century restoration, but omits the wooden lower vaulting and some of the detail of the floor of the

roof-space. It is entirely appropriate that the provenance of this model is as obscure as some aspects of the construction of the Lantern itself, and one tradition here links it to Essex's restoration in the eighteenth century.

We enter the twelfth-century spiral staircase in the northeast corner of the transept. In confirmation of its early date, we notice an exquisite top to the stone arch above the door, which displays a fishscale design. Such decoration is rarely seen inside the building but occurs again on the outside west wall of the southwest transept. On both sides of the lintel of the door are tiny bolsters or cylinders of stone, which seem to be small versions of similar devices in the arch above the monks' door (the southern entrance to the cathedral), which of course is dated to the early twelfth century. The stone surrounding us is Barnack stone brought from the very northernmost tip of present day Cambridgeshire by the Normans, even in preference to Caen stone, the stone they most often used for prestigious projects. Fortuitously, Barnack and Caen stone share

Above: The supercilium above the entrance to the choir. The tiny figure of St Mark can be seen above the arch.

Below: The twelfth century door arch

the many good characteristics of 'oolitic' limestone, and harden significantly on exposure to the weather, while transport of stone from Barnack to Ely was obviously a much more practical proposition using the rivers and waterways across the fens. Two kinds of Barnack stone have been used here at Ely. Barnack 'rag' was used for exterior work and Barnack 'oolite' for interior purposes.

Fortunately for continuity at Ely, the quarry at Barnack continued to yield good stone until the building of the new Octagon was almost complete. T. D. Atkinson[28] suggests that Weldon stone was used for the interior of the Octagon, and Barnack stone (or something very like it) for the outside facing of the Octagon.

A short clockwise spiral stair takes us to the north transept tribune (the middle storey of the cathedral), and the first things we see are the six largest of the organ pipes, lying horizontally because of their enormous length. The largest is the thirty-two-foot-long pipe that provides the considerable rumble at the base of the melody when full volume is required. In the nineteenth century the town subscribed £80 to provide the first version of this pipe alone. The present pipes here are replacements put here in the 1970s, and are part of that 'revoicing' supervised by Arthur Wills the organist here then, whose reputation still reverberates around the choir to this day. Arthur, now retired, who was known to like 'making the organ thunder', wrote a special piece to celebrate the inauguration of the new organ, and concern was expressed at the time, that the transept window adjacent to, and in direct line with the largest organ pipes, might be modified by the performance. Happily it wasn't.

This part of the cathedral is very early in date, and although the south transept is slightly older, the rather battered twelfth-century bays opposite us on the west wall of the transept have a patina of great age. Some of the columns in the top windows are clearly less than vertical, and the sill they rest on has some uncomfortable looking irregularities. John Maddison, the architectural historian, has suggested that these irregularities are remaining evidence that it was the northwest pillar of the original Norman tower that collapsed first, followed quickly by the rest of the tower.

These bays eloquently evoke thoughts of Simeon, the erstwhile Prior of Winchester, ordered to begin building the great new church at Ely in the late eleventh century. Starting the task as a venerable octogenarian, he lived to be almost a centenarian, and the similarity of our transept bays to those at Winchester suggests that Simeon himself had more than a little to do with their original

28 See T. D. Atkinson, *An Architectural History of the Benedictine Monastery of St Etheldreda at Ely*, p. 39 and footnote.

design. He had after all previously helped to draw up the plans for Winchester at the behest of his brother, Bishop Walkelin.

As our gaze moves to the right towards the north wall of the transept, we can make out slight evidence of the catastrophic collapse of the northwest corner of this transept in 1699. A jagged 'join' line at the top left of the tribune arch nearest to the north wall, and a slightly more sand tint to the Ketton stone on the right of that arch, betray the early eighteenth-century restoration of this corner of the transept by a very enlightened Dean and Chapter. They were persuaded that only exact replacement of the collapsed corner of the transept would be successful structurally and stylistically. Aided by the architect Grumbold from Cambridge and by no less a person than Sir Christopher Wren, who was consulted at the planning stage, they produced what must be one of the earliest examples of true restoration. We will see more evidence of this collapse and restoration in the early 1700s when we reach the roof, and can see their work from the outside.

Before we leave the tribune we should not omit to study the fine hammer-beam roof above us. Together with its twin on the south transept, this roof was built in the early fifteenth century, about a hundred years after the Octagon and Lantern. They replaced the steep but flatter-topped, fourteenth-century 'kerb' or mansard roofs, which were built in the 1330s to accommodate the lines of the rebuilt central tower. The redundant outlines are traced clearly on the outside walls of the Octagon tower itself, above the fifteenth-century roofline. These fifteenth-century roofs inherit the technology first explored and developed in the construction of the Lantern, so it is entirely appropriate that Ely should be the only major English cathedral to possess open hammer-beam roofs of the fifteenth century.[29] These roofs are much shallower in pitch than the original twelfth- or fourteenth-century roofs of the transepts, and have the advantage that the lead covering of the roofs needs less maintenance because at a shallower angle the lead is not so inclined to creep. (I was surprised to learn that lead is in fact a very slow moving liquid, and at steep angles it will flow downwards and if unattended will eventually curl up and fall off.) The ornate carved angels beneath the roof are in fact strong supports that provide a means by which less side thrust is placed on the parapet of the wall. Supports for the roof spring from their backs, at points well inboard of the parapet. A flatter, heavier roof can therefore be accommodated. Both transept roofs were extensively restored and repainted in the nineteenth century as part of the

29 See Harry Batsford and Charles Fry, *The Cathedrals of England* (London, B. T. Batsford, revised 1960), p. 77.

Looking eastwards from the north transept roof. The Lady chapel is to the left and the presbytery to the right. The Great Ouse flows from right to left in the middle distance. Note the black peat soil visible in the newly ploughed fields.

Victorian restoration.

Leaving the tribune, we ascend the spiral stair that takes us past the 'clerestory' level (the topmost of the transept's storeys) and out through the small door onto the transept roof, where a truly magnificent view awaits. Gripping the railing firmly, we look past the east end of the cathedral to where the fields of the fens extend almost to the horizon. These fields are only just at or about sea level and when you consider that the sea is perhaps thirty miles (forty-eight kilometres) from Ely, some idea of the proportions of the task of draining the fens can be gained. One can also reflect on how soon rising sea levels may make Ely an island once more if global warming accelerates or for any reason the pumps fall silent.

On our left as we look east is the Lady chapel, and from this vantage point we may more readily appreciate how the preparation of the ground for this huge structure in 1321 so close to the site of the central tower may have led to its collapse in 1322.

A glance behind us before we proceed across the roof will show, on the right, a very fine twelfth-century pinnacle, complete

with atavistic, blank-eyed sculptures of heads and faces, which cover the whole range from savage to silly. My own favourite is the sooty little gentleman with 'goggly' eyes, just to the left of the lightning conductor. On his left there appears to be a fair representation of Donald Duck.

In contrast, the eighteenth-century replacement pinnacle on the north-western corner of the transept has somewhat refined 'Age of Reason' faces with curious winged ears. Very obviously apparent is the join line between the twelfth- and eighteenth-century stonework at the pitch of the roof. A lead plaque proclaims that the roof lead was replaced in 1955 by Messrs Rattee and Kett. This firm started its association with the cathedral at the time of the nineteenth-century restoration by Sir George Gilbert Scott, and only recently ceased operations in April 2006.

Looking up now towards the Octagon, we can see the huge hollow tower that arose through the hole in the roof caused by the collapse. It stitched together the four damaged arms of the church and provided the reinforced centre to contain and support the Lantern. We can also trace the outlines of the lower part of the earlier twelfth-century roof of the transept.

I mentioned earlier the curious formation of *oculi* and the tops

Sculptures of heads and faces on a twelfth-century pinnacle. Note the 'sooty little gentleman with goggly eyes', and 'Donald Duck', either side of the small round window.

of the large Octagon windows and the possibility that the first stone parapet of the tower was intended to be at the string-course now just above us. The texture of the stone above and below this line is clearly very different, and it may be that our conjectural 'pause' in the building operations took place at this stage. The lancet windows which J. H. Harvey thought contained early Perpendicular elements in their design are just above our 'pause', and I find it easy to be convinced that they are later features.

Above us is the wooden Lantern covered in lead and supported on its sixteen huge supports that descend inside the stonework of the tower to their bases adjacent to the sides of the four Octagon windows. If we look now into the corner between the eastern arm of the church and the transept we are standing on, we will see the opposing flying buttresses which carry support for four of those raking shores from the sides of the window down into the column which stands immediately outside the window.

We enter the Octagon tower itself by the tiny door at the end of the transept gutters and climb the very narrow stairway that leads upward into what more resembles a chimney than a staircase. After a short and claustrophobic climb, we emerge into the roofspace of the tower, surrounded by massive beams of oak and pine.

Notice first that as you cross the threshold into the chamber you step on the rubble filling in the cavity between the inner and outer stone skins of the tower. This is one of the few places in the cathedral where the structural 'innards' of the walls and columns are to be seen by visitors. The mix of the infill seems to be limestone chips and stone waste (about forty millimetres in diameter) in lime mortar.

At the end of the walkway before us, we see the foot of one of the eight great oaks at the corner of the Lantern itself, and at just about high head height we see the two great raking shores which carry the weight of that corner down deep into the stone fabric of the tower beneath, at the level of the ends of the hood moulds of the four large windows in the Octagon. To obtain an impression of the essential simplicity of the original design we need to exclude from our mind's eye all but the eight oaks, the sixteen raking shores, the beams of the floor beneath us, and the wooden vaulting deep below. As we stand in the roof space surrounded by the stonework of the Octagon tower, we are in effect standing inside the hole in the roof caused by the collapse in 1322.

At first sight it is difficult to decide which of the many beams form the original structure that William Hurley erected. One tell-

The rubble infill in the cavity between the inner and outer walls of the Octagon tower

tale feature of the original construction is that the oak components are only roughly shaped using axes, chisels and adzes. The eighteenth-century restoration structure is composed of mechanically sawn and squared beams of oak and pine. The eight nineteenth-century additions to the structure are vertical beams easily located at the centre points of each of the eight sides of the stone tower. They provide the seats for the feet of the buttresses replaced by Scott to brace the upper Lantern against the wind.

The floor of the roof space, constructed in eight huge fans of joists radiating from each corner of the tower, are supported from below by the curved ribs of the decorative vaulting which serve to hide the utilitarian support beams from the church below. As we have already seen, there are copious carpenter's marks to suggest that the floor was made to a pattern on the ground, marked, disassembled, and reassembled at height. Notice in particular the variations of style in the joints and the letters crudely cut in the beams to identify the corners 'A' to 'H'. If you examine the lower

The foot of one of the eight great oaks at the corners of the Lantern. The lower diagonal supports are the original 'raking shores'. The supports above them are the 'Essex' duplicates.

Opposite: One of the angels of the Octagon (note the angel's very long legs)

sections of the great oaks one by one, you will find not only substantial variations of the height of the joints with the raking shores, but also that three of the great oaks seem to be divided vertically into two parts. Truly an enigma wrapped in a mystery.

We can see at a glance that there have been major modifications to the structure, mainly of course at the time of the eighteenth-century restoration. First of all, the slots in the masonry at each corner of the tower built to take the fourteenth-century supports for the roof are now empty, except for short stubs at the top of the slots to support the present roof. Stone corbels within the slots have replaced the lower parts of these posts, and they support Essex's additional framework. Secondly, the flooring joists are cut short of this corner support and are now supported on Essex's ingenious arrangement using beams across the corners between the *oculi*, and extra beams to reinforce the support for the floor. Duplicate raking shores are now in evidence and it is reasonable to surmise, I think, that they would have been vital when Essex came to replace the ends of the 'seven or eight supports that had rotted at the lower ends'. Shining a powerful torch down to the roots of those raking shores reveals what looks like the tops of the sections 'scarfed in' and clamped to the original timber.

Peering below the floor supports, to the walls below the *oculi*, you will see the sixteen stone corbels that Philip Dixon noted and which may have been part of an earlier proposed design.

Examining the vaulting beneath the main supports, we can see that it seems to be an entirely separate structure from those supports. Perhaps we will never know for certain to what extent the vaulting helps to carry the considerable weight of the Lantern. As I have already said, I find it easy to be convinced that the raking shores carry most if not all of the Lantern's bulk.

Visitors find the next part of the tour to be an outstanding highlight. To be so close to the angels they saw from the pavement of the Octagon comes as a surprise. One panel in each of the internal faces of the Lantern opens towards us into the roofspace to reveal an extremely tall angel, either playing a musical instrument or swinging an incense burner, or in one extreme example playing bagpipes. Even more impressively visitors can look down into the great internal space of the Octagon from our present height of about one hundred feet (thirty-three metres). I hasten to reassure those of a nervous disposition that we are looking over the framing of the Lantern, which at this point is above waist height, so we feel completely secure. Since, too, we are at the centre of the cross of

Looking through an open panel to the angels on the opposite side of the Lantern

the cathedral we can look down into any of the four arms of the 'cross' by opening the corresponding panel. Particularly imposing is the view down into the east end should the choir be performing or rehearsing. The sound seems to be funnelled up into the Lantern and reverberates all around the tower.

As we have already seen, Thomas Gambier Parry painted the angels in 1875 and his theme was Psalm 150:

> *Praise ye the LORD.*
> *Praise God in his sanctuary:*
> *praise him in the firmament of his power.*
> *Praise him for his mighty acts:*
> *praise him according to his excellent greatness.*
> *Praise him with the sound of the trumpet:*
> *praise him with the psaltery and harp.*
> *Praise him with the timbrel and dance:*
> *praise him with stringed instruments and organs.*
> *Praise him upon the loud cymbals:*
> *praise him upon the high sounding cymbals.*
> *Let every thing that hath breath praise the LORD.*
> *Praise ye the LORD.*

Above the angels, the windows of the Lantern bear Dean George Peacock's initials, 'G.P.', and tiny depictions of peacocks. The windows were inserted in 1863 as part of the memorial to our reforming dean who died in November 1858.

The central boss of the Lantern

We have arrived at the culmination of Alan's devotional theme, 'Christ displaying his crucifixion wounds' on the central boss of the Lantern just above us now. We know that the angels depicted in the top of the vault are most likely wholly Victorian in inspiration, but the central boss was undoubtedly placed here on the instructions of Alan himself in the late 1330s. To me it speaks plainly of our redemption, and that message has clearly survived the damage and obliteration of the Reformation. Nicola Coldstream in her analysis of the Decorated style,[30] suggests that this icon is a somewhat unusual one. She gives the example of the south door at Lincoln where a similar image is displayed and comments that 'Christ's unusual gesture pointing to the wound in his side, may be derived from Westminster Abbey'. Maybe we owe our carving to Bishop Hotham's presence in the corridors of power?

30 See Nicola Coldstream, *The Decorated Style: Architecture and Ornament, 1240-1360* (London, British Museum Press, 1994), p. 29.

In the nineteenth-century restoration of the Lantern, Scott rebuilt substantial lead-covered casings around the great oaks, replaced complex tracery in the Lantern windows, and added dummy bell louvres to the upper windows.

Leaving the roof space the same way as we entered, we ascend the short staircase to the roof of the Octagon tower. We are now on the leaded roof at the foot of the Lantern, and can see the Lantern at close quarters. It seems to me that the nineteenth-century intention 'to return the Octagon and Lantern to something like their mediaeval form' was very effectively carried out as far as we are able to say. If we examine the pinnacles on top of the eight stairwells, we can discern a change in the texture of the stonework some three or four courses above the mediaeval string-course where Sir George Gilbert Scott provided the decorated pinnacles that the mediaeval builders had not got round to providing in the

In the centre is a pinnacle provided by Scott on top of a mediaeval stairhead tower. To the left is one of the slender nineteenth-century pinnacles built in the centre of the long sides of the Octagon tower to take the thrust of the reinserted buttresses (right).

first build and Essex seems to have omitted from his planned schedule in the eighteenth century. The four slender square-section pinnacles at the centre of each of the longer sides of the tower were entirely added by the Victorians to take the stresses imposed by the renewal of the large buttresses to the sides of the Lantern, and formed no part of the original mediaeval design.

The louvred windows to the bell chamber, provided as part of the nineteenth-century scheme, are of course only dummies, because the Lantern has not contained bells since 1670 or so.

On a routine tour of the Octagon, we would normally complete the exercise with a slow and careful circuit of the tower pointing

Right: The climb completed! The great oak and the ladder are in the inside corner of the casing, beneath my boot. The triangular 'squeeze' point is clearly visible below!

Opposite: The west tower from the roof of the Lantern

out the many points of interest below. Since however this is clearly a virtual tour, and virtual visitors do not need the protection of the Ecclesiastical Insurance Company, I propose that I take you to the very top of the Lantern.

We enter the fabric of the Lantern itself by a small inspection door in one of the lead casings and in the corner we see a ladder fixed to the surface of the great oak. The treads of the ladder are very slim and only provide a toehold, but the frame of the casing is near enough to our backs to enable us to sit on the horizontal bars occasionally when we need to draw breath. After ascending for about thirty feet (nine metres), hugging the ladder close, we reach a narrower section where the framing of the Lantern intrudes on our narrow shaft in the form of a triangle of beams that we must squeeze through. The final ten feet or so is relatively plain sailing and we reach a small door which opens in the side of the casing and scramble out onto the very top of the Lantern surrounded by the eight little turrets and the fancy balustrade.

We are at about a hundred and seventy feet (fifty-two metres) or so above the ground and in moving a few paces around the tower top we can see the entire bulk of the cathedral below us. To stand on the little octagonal lead boss at the centre of that roof is to enjoy a truly spectacular widescreen view. Our circle of visibility is probably around thirty miles (forty-eight kilometres) across. Only the west tower peers down on our vantage point, but we can

Above left: Section of the roof structure of the Lantern. The trapdoor and the ladder down into the bell chamber are seen right of centre.

Above right: The central roof support in the centre of the empty bell chamber. The side of the ladder is to the left of the picture. The covered windows are the louvred bell windows.

nevertheless see daylight through its topmost windows.

Moving across the roof to the large and heavy lead covered trapdoor we lift it and descend into the dark and dusty chamber that held the bells until their hurried removal in 1670. The chamber is now entirely empty but the louvres of the windows provide homes for some of the many jackdaws that populate our towers.

Retracing our steps up the bell chamber ladder, down the narrow casing, past the slightly alarming pinch point in the framing, we are fully occupied in keeping ourselves safe. When we reach the comparative security of the Octagon roof, however, we have time to look down over Ely itself, and ponder all we have seen—a truly beautiful structure that nevertheless hugely impresses with its mechanical efficiency and its ingenuity. Built to the glory of God, and with a deep religious significance to its own era that we can only partly see, I am convinced that the 'three triumphs' are an apt summing up. A triumph over adversity, a triumph of friendship and co-operation, and finally a triumph of innovation.

I can assure you that when you have seen the Octagon for yourself, you will agree that it is a 'promise of beauty' fulfilled.

Some Frequently Asked Questions

How many casualties were there when the tower collapsed?
Anglia Sacra (H. Wharton, see Select Bibliography) says 'no-one was hurt or crushed by the fall of the tower' ('*neminem tamen laedens nec opprimens in ruina*').

Why did the old tower fall?
We are in the realms of theory here. Professor J. Heyman (*The Stone Skeleton*, Cambridge, Cambridge University Press, 1997) suggests that the building of the Lady chapel—started in 1321—caused alterations in the water table beneath the tower. Philip Dixon, the cathedral archaeologist, also tells of deep trenches dug under the cathedral in antiquity to help drain the considerable springs which would otherwise have 'pooled' under the building. Parts of the Lady chapel foundations incorporate arches to allow water to escape.

Were many people hurt or killed in the building of the Octagon and the Lantern?
The simple truth is we just don't know. There are no clues in the records we have for some eleven years of the total twenty years or so of the construction period. My own feeling is that these 'sacrist rolls' would have mentioned any exceptional provision for casualties or more likely their families. Elsewhere, for example, it is recorded faithfully that Alan paid for treatment for one of his grooms who had been severely hurt by Alan's horse.

How were the Octagon and Lantern decorated originally?
We have only the sketchiest of descriptions in the literature. We must remember that the original scheme disappeared under limewash, probably at some time during the eighteenth century,

and only reappeared in 1850 when the Victorians scraped off the limewash. The faint mediaeval traces of paintwork revealed were described thus in an 1880 guidebook:

> The pattern was a series of quatrefoils, painted in stone colour on the wood, outlined black, and filled with green. The bosses of the Lantern, which are not carved, had been evidently painted and gilt, but the patterns of foliage were rough and too much injured to afford any distinct composition. The small amount of colouring that remained on some of the mouldings of the Octagon was principally of a bright red, but only in small patches, the groundwork having peeled off and the colour with it.

Sadly in 1875 all trace of the mediaeval work was obliterated by Thomas Gambier Parry's rather heavyweight 'spirit fresco' paint. Otherwise known as 'the Ely medium', its formula was as follows:

> One part pale drying oil; one part strong copal varnish; two parts japanner's gold size; two parts turpentine, and the powder colours to be ground up in the medium.

He carried out all his work at Ely in this medium.

What was painted on the 'angel doors' in the Lantern, before the present Victorian angels?

Again we don't know anything for certain. All the earlier pictures of the Lantern show either limewash or blank doors. One early photo in Gerald Cobb's *English Cathedrals the Forgotten Centuries* (Thames and Hudson, 1980, plate 138) shows apparently open spaces where the opening panels are now, 'after Scott had completed his work on the choir screen'. It occurs to me that the panels were missing because Parry was actually painting them at the time. It seems clear from the 1874 guidebook that the angels were Parry's own original thought on the theme of Psalm 150 (see page 98).

Which of the great oaks is hollowed up the inside so that you can climb up to the top by the ladder?

This question is asked surprisingly often. There seems to be a deep-rooted belief in Ely that the eight great oaks entirely fill the lead-covered casings at each corner of the Lantern, as seen from the ground. The answer is of course that the ladder in question is fixed to the side of one of the oaks, and the oak ascends in one corner of the square casing.

Why Lantern? Was it to guide people across the fens?

I think the answer is that the Lantern was intended only to light the centre of the crossing with additional light. I usually tell the questioner that on only one occasion was it intended that the Lantern would provide light instead of just receiving it. In 1802, a carpenter intent on celebrating a European peace treaty suggested that a wooden chandelier be constructed and hoisted up into the Lantern ablaze with candles. You can guess what happened. The wreckage was hurriedly tossed down into the crossing and extinguished (see Peter Moore, *Three Restorations of Ely Cathedral*, Dean & Chapter of Ely, 1973, p. 13).

Some Vital Statistics at Ely Cathedral

Exterior dimensions

Opposite: The west front of Ely Cathedral

	feet	(metres)
Exterior length from west to east	537	(165)
Total length of eastern transept from north to south	190	(58)
Total height of the four west tower stone turrets	215	(66)
Height of the roof over the nave	104	(32)
Height of the Lantern over the dome	170	(52)
Height of the eastern front to the top of the cross	112	(34)

Interior dimensions

	feet	(metres)
Height from Octagon paving to central boss	142	(44)
Crossing the Octagon	71	(22)
Clear diameter of the Lantern within	30	(9)
Height of the Lantern from the aperture in the dome to the upper vaulting	48	(15)
Height of the vaulted roof of the choir	70	(22)
Height of the nave ceiling at the east end	86	(26)

Select Bibliography

Atkinson, T. D., *An Architectural History of the Benedictine Monastery of St Etheldreda at Ely* (Cambridge, Cambridge University Press, 1933).

Bentham, James, *The History and Antiquities of the Conventual & Cathedral Church of Ely* (Cambridge, Cambridge University Press, 1812).

Chapman, F. R., *Sacrist Rolls of Ely, 2 vols* (Cambridge, Cambridge University Press, 1908).

Coldstream, Nicola, *The Decorated Style: Architecture and Ornament, 1240-1360* (London, British Museum Press, 1994).

Coneybeare, Edward, *Highways and Byways in Cambridge and Ely* (London, Macmillan, 1910).

Evans, Seiriol J. A., ed., *Ely Chapter Ordinances and Visitation Records 1241-1515*, Camden Miscellany, 16 (London, Royal Historical Society, 1940).

Fairweather, Janet, *Liber Eliensis: A History of the Isle of Ely from the Seventh Century to the Twelfth Compiled by a Monk of Ely in the Twelfth Century* (Woodbridge, Boydell, 2005).

Fletcher, John, 'Medieval Timberwork at Ely', in *Medieval Art and Architecture at Ely Cathedral: The British Archaeological Association Conference Transactions for the Year 1976*, ed. Nicola Coldstream and Peter Draper ([London], British Archaeological Association, 1979).

Fuller, Thomas, *The History of the Worthies of England* (London, 1662), in *Early English Books Online* <http://eebo.chadwyck.com>.

Opposite: A view of Bishop's House from the very top of the Lantern—formerly the great hall of the priory in monastic days

Goodich, Michael E., *Violence and Miracle in the Fourteenth Century: Private Grief and Public Salvation* (Chicago, The University of Chicago Press, 1995).

Harvey, John H., *Henry Yevele c.1320 to 1400: The Life of an English Architect* (London, Batsford, 1944).

Hewett, Cecil A., *English Cathedral and Monastic Carpentry* (Chichester, Phillimore, 1985).

Heyman, Jacques, *The Stone Skeleton: Structural Engineering of Masonry Architecture* (Cambridge, Cambridge University Press, 1997).

Lindley, Phillip, 'The Imagery of the Octagon at Ely', *Journal of the British Archaeological Association*, 139 (1986), pp 75–99.

Lindley, Phillip, 'The Fourteenth-Century Architectural Programme at Ely Cathedral', in *England in the Fourteenth Century: Proceedings of the 1985 Harlaxton Symposium*, ed. W. M. Ormrod (Woodbridge, Boydell Press, 1986), pp 119–129.

Lindley, Phillip, 'Carpenter's Gothic and gothic carpentry', *Journal of the Society of Architectural Historians of Great Britain*, 30 (1987), pp 83–112.

Maddison, John, *Ely Cathedral: Design and Meaning* (Ely, Ely Cathedral Publications, 2000).

Stenton, Frank, *Anglo-Saxon England* (Oxford, Oxford University Press, 1971).

Stewart, D. J., *On the Architectural History of Ely Cathedral* (London, J. Van Voorst, 1868).

Stubbs, C. W., *Historical Memorials of Ely Cathedral* (London, J. M. Dent & Co., 1897).

Wade, E. C., and Heyman, Professor J., 'The Timber Octagon of Ely Cathedral', *Institution of Civil Engineers (Great Britain) Proceedings. Part I*, 78 (Dec. 1985), pp 1421–1436 (Paper No. P8895).

Wharton, Henry, *Anglia Sacra, sive, Collectio Historiarum ... de Archiepiscopis et Episcopis Angliæ, a prima fidei Christianæ susceptione ad annum 1540; Nunc primum in lucem editarum* (Londini, 1691), in *Early English Books Online* <http://eebo.chadwyck.com>.

Index

As one of Ely Cathedral's specialist guides, Michael White has shown thousands of visitors around Ely's Octagon Tower and Lantern, the unique and ingenious fourteenth-century structure that forms the Cathedral's magnificent centrepiece. In *A Promise of Beauty* he offers an engaging and accessible account of the Octagon's history, from the disastrous collapse of the Norman tower that once stood in its place through to the extensive restoration work that modified its form in the eighteenth and nineteenth centuries. Basing his narrative in part upon an exhaustive examination of surviving written sources, he also provides an intimate and revealing first-hand appraisal of the Octagon Tower as it stands today, offering new insights into the intentions of its creator, Alan of Walsingham, and shedding new light on some of its enduring mysteries.

ISBN 978-0-9555777-0-3

9 780955 577703

UK: £9.99

www.FrameCharge.com

Pilates for
EQUESTRIANS

Achieve the winning edge with increased core stability

LIZA RANDALL